I'm Still With You

© John Elkins

About the Author

Sherrie Dillard is an internationally renowned psychic, medium, medical intuitive, and best-selling author. She has given over 65,000 readings worldwide. She has been featured on radio and television as a medium and medical intuitive, including national television for her work in assisting police detectives in solving the Stephanie Bennett cold case murder.

Sherrie has a degree in psychology and an MDiv in metaphysics and New Thought pastoral counseling. She has taught intuition and spiritual development classes at Duke University, at Miraval Resort, and in Europe, Costa Rica, and Mexico. Her passion for the fusion of intuition, spirituality, and conscious self-growth has made her a popular speaker and teacher.

Sherrie Dillard

I'm Still With You

Communicate, Heal & Evolve *with* *Your* Loved One *on* *the* Other Side

Llewellyn Publications
Woodbury, Minnesota

First Edition
Sixth Printing, 2023

Cover design by Shira Atapku
Editing by Hanna Grimson

Llewellyn Publications is a registered trademark of Llewellyn Worldwide Ltd.

Library of Congress Cataloging-in-Publication Data
Names: Dillard, Sherrie,
Title: I'm still with you: communicate, heal & evolve with your loved one on the other side / Sherrie Dillard.
Description: First edition. | Woodbury, Minnesota: Llewellyn Publications, 2020. | Includes bibliographical references. | Summary: "Psychic medium Sherrie Dillard shares case studies that show how the power of love transcends the veil between this world and the next. This book features exercises and meditations for working through grief and continuing communication with family and friends who have passed over. It provides examples of what loved ones encounter after passing over and guides readers into a soul-to-soul journey with family and friends on the other side"—Provided by publisher.
Identifiers: LCCN 2019058958 (print) | LCCN 2019058959 (ebook) | ISBN 9780738761367 (paperback) | ISBN 9780738761718 (ebook)
Subjects: LCSH: Spiritualism.
Classification: LCC BF1261.2 .D49 2020 (print) | LCC BF1261.2 (ebook) | DDC 133.9/1—dc23
LC record available at https://lccn.loc.gov/2019058958
LC ebook record available at https://lccn.loc.gov/2019058959

Llewellyn Worldwide Ltd. does not participate in, endorse, or have any authority or responsibility concerning private business transactions between our authors and the public.

All mail addressed to the author is forwarded but the publisher cannot, unless specifically instructed by the author, give out an address or phone number.

Any internet references contained in this work are current at publication time, but the publisher cannot guarantee that a specific location will continue to be maintained. Please refer to the publisher's website for links to authors' websites and other sources.

Llewellyn Publications
A Division of Llewellyn Worldwide Ltd.
2143 Wooddale Drive
Woodbury, MN 55125-2989
www.llewellyn.com

Printed in the United States of America

Other Books by Sherrie Dillard

You Are a Medium

You Are Psychic

Develop Your Medical Intuition

Discover Your Psychic Type

Discover Your Authentic Self

The Miracle Workers Handbook

Love and Intuition

Sacred Signs & Symbols

I've Never Met a Dead Person I Didn't Like

The stories included in this book are true accounts taken from my personal life and reading sessions. The names and other identifying characteristics of individuals have been changed to protect anonymity. Any similarities to a known person are coincidental and unintentional.

Dedication

Dedicated to the noble Busta, now running like a crazy boy in the skies. To Kenni, who is right alongside him, enjoying the harmony of the celestial and its rhythms.

To all of my clients' family, friends, and loved ones on the other side who have communicated with me. Thank you for choosing me.

Disclaimer

The material in this book is not intended as a substitute for trained medical or psychological advice. Readers are advised to consult their personal healthcare professionals regarding treatment. The publisher and the author assume no liability for any injuries or mental health issues that may result from the reader's use of the content contained herein and recommend common sense when contemplating the practices described in the work.

Acknowledgments

I'd like to thank the devoted people of Llewellyn, especially Angela Wix, Hanna Grimson, Kat Sanborn, and all the wonderful supportive folks who helped bring this book to fruition. Immense gratitude for everything you all do to continue to fill the world with books of wonder.

Special thanks to Kenni, who encouraged me to share the information in this book with others. You continue to inspire and keep things interesting for me from the other side.

Contents

Exercises and Meditations

Chapter 13

Introduction

When a Loved One Passes Over

Not long ago, I taught a workshop on how to communicate with the other side. In this experiential class, students learned how to intuitively connect with their own and others' family and friends on the other side. Over the course of my thirty-plus years as a medium, I've taught this class many times. However, as I stood in the front of the room that Sunday afternoon, I could feel that something was different. As I explained various spiritual concepts and the mechanics of communicating with the other side, I felt something or someone pull my attention away from the class and into the spirit realm. This was not a gentle nudge but a "pay attention to me" kind of spirit intrusion. Not wanting to take time away from my students, I did my best to stay focused, and fortunately this spirit interruption didn't seem to affect others.

On my way home the spirit presence that I felt during the class came closer and felt stronger. During the ninety-minute drive, I talked to this spirit and asked him such things as, "What happened?" and "How was your passing?"

As this presence drew closer, I felt a tugging in my heart, and I found myself spontaneously expressing my love for him. In return I felt his warmth and love, and tears came to my eyes. As strange as this may sound, I knew that I was talking to my ex-husband. However, even though I "knew" that his spirit was with me, I wasn't ready to acknowledge that he had passed over. As far as I knew he was healthy and alive in the physical world. The shock of seeing and feeling his spirit close was more than I was able to accept. So, I continued this conversation in as much denial as I could muster.

Later that evening, I received a message from one of the students in the class. He told me that he didn't want to intrude into my personal life, but he felt compelled to reach out and tell me that he felt a male spirit close to me during the class.

"He seemed to be trying to get your attention," he said.

I acknowledged his astute, intuitive observation and told him that I felt him too.

The next morning, I received a phone call from a friend letting me know that Kenni, my ex-husband, had died the afternoon before. His time of death coincided with the start of my class and unbeknownst to me, we were just a few miles apart at the time.

Like others who suffer a loss, I felt a flood of emotions and unanswered questions crowd into my mind. Unlike a television sitcom where the loose ends are neatly woven together to make for a satisfying ending, his passing left me feeling incomplete. There were feelings and emotions that hadn't been expressed and unresolved issues that I knew we both needed to work through.

Over the course of my professional career as a medium, I've given readings to many who feel the same way. When a loved one passes over, we are often overwhelmed with emotion. Along with emotions such as grief, shock, and confusion, we may not be ready to let go. The relationship may not feel complete, and we might feel that we need more time with our loved one. Perhaps we haven't expressed all that is in our heart, or it might feel as if something has been left undone. There may have been a shared higher purpose, lesson, or gift that wasn't actualized, or we may regret not making the most of our time together. When we feel as if we have failed to fully reconcile our differences with another, it can be challenging to find peace with ourselves.

Death can feel like the end. When a loved one dies, they seem gone forever and out of our reach. We may cling to all that we shared with them and hold on tightly to past memories in an attempt to keep them close. We may wonder where they are, what they are experiencing, and if they can see and sense us.

However, even when we are not aware that our loved one, family member, or friend is close, they are, perhaps even looking right at us and likely trying to get our attention. Love between souls doesn't diminish with passing. Not only is our love eternal, our bond and connection with those we love survives physical death.

Why We Seek Mediums

Many of my clients are spurred to have a medium reading because of the loss of a loved one. Some may not have previously thought much about communicating with the other side, yet their grief and sadness and the sense that their loved one may be close compels them to reach out in any way possible. Some have felt the presence of a loved one in a dream or noticed signs such as pennies on their path or a bird that continuously sits on their window ledge, and they wonder if their loved one is trying to get their attention or send them a message.

Despite our grief and anguish over losing a loved one, in our deepest heart we may sense that they are close. The soft whispers that they are still a part of us and we are a part of them resound even within our doubts. Yet, we may not know how to bridge the gap between realms. When a loved one passes over, we can no longer rely on text messages, emails, or other forms of more worldly communication. Instead, we are confronted with the task of finding out if there is a way to slip under the curtain between realms.

In the physical world we often define our relationships by our shared everyday activities, goals, common beliefs, and how we feel in another's presence. When we do things together, share intimacies, discuss our thoughts and feelings, express our love, and seek to understand one another, our bond with them strengthens and feels more solid. However, there is also something undefinable that exists between ourselves and those we love. It is not easy to fully grasp and put into words the special something we feel and experience in their presence. This magnet-like current seems to draw us to one another and keeps us loving and devoted to them despite how challenging the relationship may be.

When a loved one passes over, that not-so-easy-to-identify invisible something is what we are left with. It is an energy, a pull, a feeling and connection, a magical synergy. In our connectedness with a friend, lover, partner, or family member, we are someone different than who we are when we are alone. When a loved one transitions, we not only grieve their passing, we also miss a part of ourselves.

Memories of our loved ones often bring us comfort and sustain us. Through recalling shared events and special moments, we resurrect what was and remember parts of ourselves. The past becomes a safe and loving haven as well as a link to our loved one and the life that now may seem to be gone forever.

Dwelling on memories is a natural and necessary part of the grieving process. However, if we stay too long and get overly focused on the past, we miss out on the very real present where the activity of our life is taking place. We also miss out on the opportunity to discover that the special something that exists between ourselves and our loved one is still present. Even though we may feel raw, vulnerable, and alone, there is often a sliver of recognition that they are somehow close, maybe by our side, and still loving us.

As comforting as it may be, the idea that it is possible that a loved one is alive and present may not always be easy to accept. The thought that there is life after death and that we can communicate with the other side can feel a bit daunting and beyond our reach.

Intuitive Awareness on the Other Side Is Immediate

Although we may hesitate to accept that those in the spirit realm can reach out and be with us, our loved ones on the other side are experiencing something quite different. For those in the spirit realm, communicating with loved ones still in the physical world is more straightforward and uncomplicated. Even if they had no interest in intuition while here in the physical world, this is now the natural way that they communicate. It is not something that they believe or don't believe is possible; it just is. They see us and are aware of our thoughts and feelings and long to let us know that they are close.

The other side is not as distant and beyond our grasp as we may believe. It is an integral aspect of our wholeness and the home of our loved ones who have passed over. When a loved one leaves the physical world, our bond with them still exists. Even though they are no longer in the body and we can't do all of the things with them that brought us joy and gave us comfort, our connection with them is still valuable.

On the other side, our loved ones continue to support and love those they left behind. They have ascended into a higher state of love and wisdom and perceive us through this enlightened awareness. They are able to better understand the purpose and soulful meaning of our relationship with them, and they celebrate the joy and support they shared with us. The mystery of their connection with those they were close to in the physical world has both deepened and been revealed.

Where the Information Comes From

This book offers new insights and information about what your loved ones on the other side are likely experiencing and how to communicate, grow, and evolve along with them. It will open you to new possibilities and avenues to explore within yourself and with those on the other side.

For over thirty-five years I've communicated with those on the other side and witnessed the healing and transformation that often occurs when we become open to the possibility of connecting to our loved ones who have passed on. This book serves as a guide to better understanding the rich and varied life that our loved ones are creating and experiencing on the other side. It provides suggestions to help you move through the grieving process and guides you into a transformative soul-to-soul journey with your loved one.

Throughout the book there are case studies taken from my almost four decades of experience as a medium. From people who may not have believed in life after death to those who intuitively prepared themselves to communicate with their loved ones before passing over, the stories span a wide spectrum of experiences. These accounts of how others dealt with grief and loss and were able to heal and continue their soul journey with their loved ones illustrate the guiding power and force of love that is at work after a loved one passes over.

Although I've been communicating with those on the other side for many years, I'm still surprised at times by the information that I receive. When I'm perplexed and need more clarification as to the broader meaning of what a client's loved one on the other side has communicated, I turn to my spirit guides. They help to fill in the blanks so that I can better understand the vast intricacies and possibilities of life beyond the physical world. I share these insights with you so that you too can benefit from the healing and enlightened awareness that your loved ones may be experiencing. As you explore the wonders of the limitless realm of spirit, a deep and abiding peace and connection with the other side will fill your heart and soul.

(In my books *You Are a Medium* and *I've Never Met a Dead Person I Didn't Like*, I introduce my spirit guides and describe my early childhood encounters with the other side and my work as a professional medium.)

Support for Your Journey

Through the rich, interwoven connections that we continually share with our loved ones on the other side, we are continually being influenced and guided. As our loved ones are welcomed into the light of the heavens, we may find ourselves in the midst of the grieving process feeling lost and not sure where to turn or what to do. However, it doesn't matter if you've had a recent loss or if your loved one passed over some time ago; you can heal and move forward knowing that your loved ones are close by and with you every step of the way.

While our loved ones undergo the profound transformation of passing over, we begin the long and often arduous journey through loss and grief. It winds us through unknown territory where we navigate our way through an emotional depth that we might not be familiar with. Grief changes us, and despite its difficulties and challenges, it can also herald a time of increased awareness, spiritual renewal, and the opportunity to open ourselves to the vastness of love beyond form.

To help you better understand what your loved one is experiencing, and to support you in this journey of healing and transformation, the book is divided into three sections: Living in the Wonder of the Other Side; Lifting the Curtain: Communication Between the Realms; and Transforming, Healing, and Evolving.

Living in the Wonder of the Other Side

In the first section, our loved one leaves the physical world and enters the spirit realm. Although everyone's death experience is unique, there are some commonalities. You will discover what your loved one likely encountered when they passed over and what they may be experiencing as they make their entry into the spirit realm. You'll also learn simple practices you can do that will help your loved one during and after passing and aid them in making their way into the light of the heavens.

Soon after passing over our loved ones experience the soul review. For some, this process seems to occur spontaneously and quickly. Others experience the soul review as a series of insights, awareness, and heart-opening expansion. However, this activity can't be measured in earth time as the other side is always operating in the "now" outside of time.

Through this loving and transformative process, our loved one becomes aware of how their actions, choices, and decisions impacted their soul plan and affected those that they love. The soul review differs from soul to soul. You'll gain insight into what the soul review is like for children, for those who pass over from suicide or drug overdose, and for those who bring joy or knowingly cause pain to others.

During the soul review our loved ones become aware of the soul contracts they shared with others and have the opportunity to better understand why things happened the way that they did. The soul review is not a judgment, a fault finding, or a way to incur shame and blame for misguided mistakes while in the physical world. Instead, it is an opportunity to become and be who they truly are. As our loved ones go through the soul review and awaken to their true self, they are able to positively influence and guide us.

After the soul review, our loved ones live in an enlightened awareness. They see, feel, and know us through this transformed perspective and continue to reach out to guide us along our path. As they become aware of the opportunities and possibilities available to them in the spirit realm, new aspects of their divine individuality emerge. In addition to having fun and socializing, our loved ones may choose to continue to learn and become involved in soul group activities and service and creative projects.

Lifting the Curtain: Communication Between the Realms

During the difficult time after a loved one passes over, our grief and sense of loss can be overwhelming. It may feel as if a part of us has been torn away. In this raw and vulnerable time, many experience a surprising glimmer of hope when they sense or feel that their loved one may be near. When we embrace this hope instead of dismissing it, we begin the journey of interacting and communicating across the divide between the physical and spiritual realms.

As our loved ones leave the physical body, they become aware that death is not the end. On the other side they are able to see, feel, and draw close to those they love in the physical world, and they attempt to let us know that they are with us in a variety of ways. Although they are not always successful in delivering clear and understandable messages, they eventually become better at getting our attention.

In this section you'll gain insight into the common and more unusual ways that our loved ones reach out to us and how to better identify and decipher their messages. Communication sent to us from the other side often surfaces in ways that are not always easy to notice and detect. For instance, when a loved one on the other side goes through the soul review, we too may spontaneously recall memories and receive surprising insights about ourselves and our relationship. Through messages of forgiveness, love, and healing, our loved ones extend to us the power and influence that the light of the heavens has had on them. Although we may not always be aware of their presence, the comfort and peace that they offer can lessen our grief and open us to deeper levels of self-understanding and inner healing.

You will find that intuitively receiving and sending messages with your loved ones is unlike the kind of communication you may have seen or heard of professional mediums engaging in. Connecting with your own loved ones is more emotional and heart centered than the objective information seeking of a professional medium. You don't need to be an advanced intuitive or medium to receive and share. When we pass over, we are immediately psychic, as intuition springs from our soul. Your loved ones are aware of the messages you send and do their best to let you know that they are still with you.

Interaction and communion between the physical and spiritual realms is more natural and occurs more often than we might initially realize. Through insights and exercises you will be better able to recognize the presence of your loved ones and receive the love, guidance, and healing they offer. As you become more comfortable with the unique intuitive language that you now share, you will feel closer and benefit from this interactive union.

Transforming, Healing, and Evolving

As your loved one on the other side evolves and transforms, so can you. There is a lot we can learn from the soul review about how to live a more joy-filled and peaceful life here in the physical world. It is through the soul review process that occurs soon after passing that emotional burdens and misunderstandings are acknowledged and released. As earthly perceptions are let go, insight into the purpose and gifts that the physical life provided comes to light. We live in the pureness of our soul and enter into the full experience of divine freedom, love, and wisdom.

In this section you'll have insight into the lessons that the soul review offers and how to apply them to everyday life challenges and experiences. Through questions and meditations, you'll also be guided through a mini soul review where you can discover the essential and often unrecognized purpose that a loved one has brought into your life. In the physical world we do our best to love and support our family, friends, and partners. However, our relationships can at times be challenging and bring our emotional wounds and what is in need of healing within us to the surface. There is a soul plan that isn't always evident or obvious that underlies our connections with the important people in our life. When a loved one passes over, we might feel as if we haven't resolved our issues or that something has been left undone. However, once on the other side, our loved ones are able to know and see with pure clarity and can support our awareness and healing.

In this section, you'll learn about the soul contracts that you share with your loved ones and be able to heal confusing or challenging emotional patterns. The exercises can be applied to loved ones, relatives, and friends that you were close to, as well as more distant ancestors on the other side who you may not have known well or at all. Becoming aware of and clearing limiting emotional and family patterns not only frees us, it also heals our past and future as well as the experiences of past generations and the lives of those who will come after us. When we experience healing and resolution from unsatisfying and repetitive relationship patterns, we cease creating and repeating the same unsatisfying connections with others over and over. We are truly free and create more joy and loving connections.

Your time on earth is precious and there are new experiences and ways of being for you to explore. Your loved ones on the other side are supporting your endeavors, nudging you forward, setting up opportunities for you to be in the right place at the right time, opening doors, and generally being a force of positivity in your life. The other side is not as distant and out of our reach as we may believe. It is an integral aspect of our wholeness, and we can become more conscious of the ongoing eternal relationships that we share with those in the spirit realm.

Section I

Living in the Wonder of the Other Side

Chapter 1

The Transition from
This World to the Next

The moment of our passing out of the physical body and into the spirit realm is a holy and intimate encounter with creative life force energy and truth. It doesn't matter the cause of our passing, the reason for leaving this earth, or the quality of our life; the doors to an all-encompassing love swing open. The heaviness of our troubles, worries, and suffering falls away and we float in the soft rays of light.

When someone close to us passes over, we may feel a wide range of emotions and reactions. For those who watched a loved one suffer through a long-term illness, the passing may be bittersweet. We may feel relieved that our loved one is no longer in pain and suffering. However, we still feel a tremendous amount of grief and loss. When a loved one's passing over is sudden and unexpected, we often experience shock, become numb, and perhaps go into denial. It may take time to fully feel and understand the tremendous change that has taken place in our lives. Whatever the circumstances of a loved one's passing, the life that we have been living is forever altered.

Over the course of our relationships with those we love, we energetically bond. As we spend time together and share our thoughts, emotions, and love, our connection becomes stronger. Our life experiences, emotions, and thoughts harmonize, and our spirits become intertwined. From the physical perspective, we are in separate bodies with a clear division and boundary between ourselves and another. From the spiritual energy framework, we are not as separate as what we may think. Our energy fields, or auras, and our souls are often inter-woven, come together, intermingle, and flow into oneness with one another.

Although the phrase "The whole is greater than the sum of its parts" is at-tributed to the ancient Greek philosopher Aristotle, there is no text that links him to the quote directly. However, we do know that Aristotle wrote about this phenomenon. The change and transformation that occurs when things and people come together has been continually observed since his lifetime, sometime around 350 BCE. Since at least the middle of the nineteenth cen-tury the term "synergy" began to be used in the field of physiology to describe this same sentiment. Synergy describes a phenomenon in which the combined energy of two or more parts creates something wholly new that transcends the original combination of the two.

The idea of synergy is applied in areas such as psychology and the study of behavior, business, biology, and other sciences. In psychology we find a simi-lar type of understanding in Gestalt theory, which maintains that the whole is something else or something different than its parts. We experience this phe-nomenon in our relationships. Through our loving connections with others, we are changed and become someone different. We fall in love or are attracted to a particular person because of how we feel when we are with them. We are transformed. They bring out the best, most loving, fun, and interesting parts of us. In the glow of this recognition, we become our best selves.

After a loved one passes over, we may feel raw, vulnerable, and disoriented, as if a part of us has been torn away. Although the very real and tangible bond that we feel with another is still present, we need time to transform and heal and become familiar with who we are without our loved one's physical pres-ence. In addition to the deep sadness we feel, we might also experience a sense of being not altogether present, spacey, low-energy, depressed, or lost.

Our synergistic bond with others extends beyond our feelings of affection for them. Love energetically connects us to others. When we love another and share ourselves with him or her, our energy fields unite and fuse together al-most as one. Although we still retain our individual energy field, our loved one becomes a part of us. This synergy of love transforms us. This is true in all our relationships and is most potent in our connection with those closest to us, such as our husband or wife, romantic partner, parents, children, and other close family members and friends.

The Other Side Is Eager to Communicate

The longing to connect with a loved one who has passed over often motivates those who are grieving to have a session with me. When a loved one passes over, our synergistic love cocoon becomes tattered and broken. No longer huddled close together within this energetic web of love, we long to feel their presence. Our connection with our loved one still exists, but it feels less tangible and more out of reach, and this can feel lonely, scary, and uncomfortable. Many wonder where their loved one is and if they are still suffering. The uncertainty of what may be happening on the other side often increases suffering. Even if they had not previously been interested in or curious about consulting a medium, those left behind reach out in the hope of a spiritual reunion with their loved one.

As soon as our loved ones pass out of the physical body, and quite often before they pass over, they become aware that death is not the end. Once on the other side they are able to see us and feel the shock and grief that we are experiencing. Quite often they try to let us know that they are still alive and with us. They may be eager to communicate with those they left behind and attempt to let us know that they are with us in a variety of different ways.

Our loved ones on the other side want us to know that passing over is painless and not at all as scary as what it may seem. The most frightening part of death, it seems, is our human perception of what we imagine it to be. From our earthbound perspective, the process of death usually involves fear, pain, anguish, and suffering. However, appearances can be deceiving. When the body dies, the soul takes over the reins of life and guides us into a state of being and awareness where we no longer experience fear, pain, or suffering.

At physical death we wake to our true essence and become aware of the divine beauty that we are all inherently a part of. Although we don't necessarily hear trumpets and see the pearly gates of heaven, an all-encompassing love and peace surrounds us. After passing over, most are greeted by their loved ones already on the other side and by angelic beings. Our loved ones often describe waking up in a sublime and peaceful garden where they can rest and adjust to this new celestial reality.

For instance, I had a session recently with Roger, a kind forty-nine-year-old dentist. For the past few years I had been working with Marlene, his wife. After being cancer free for several years, Marlene was told during a routine visit that her cancer had come back. Soon after returning to treatment, her doctors informed her that the chemotherapy and radiation were no longer effective. However, this didn't deter Marlene. She researched alternative healing modalities, worked with holistic health professionals, healers, and shamans, and did everything that she could to heal and stay in this world. It was during this time that she came to see me to hear from her angels and her loved ones on the other side. A few months after we began, we both became aware that those in the spirit realm were preparing her for her new life on the other side.

One afternoon after trying to contact Marlene about an upcoming session, her husband told me that she had passed over a week earlier and asked me if he could use her session to talk to her. As soon as I sat down with Roger to do the reading, Marlene came in. A luminous glow surrounded her, and she looked beautiful. Despite her young age and desire to stay in the physical world with her kind husband, Marlene accepted her transition and was at peace. She thanked her husband for sitting by her bed day and night, rubbing her feet, and being present. When the angels peacefully lifted her out of her body, she was ready and wanted Roger to know that she was always close by.

The love between Marlene and her husband was strong and undeniable. As we continued the session, they laughed about the fun and adventures they shared and the intimate last year of her life. When we finished the session, Roger quietly asked if we could speak again in a few months.

Over the course of the year that I spoke with Roger, I witnessed him move through the process of grief and come to terms with his life without his wife. Some days were more challenging than others, and he often felt the presence of Marlene close by, watching over and guiding him.

Just as Marlene was entering a new juncture of her soul journey, so was Roger. The transition from physical life to the other side is a new beginning both for those who pass over and for those they leave behind. Although we rarely realize it, we often do this work together.

Death Doesn't Feel Like Death

The circumstances of a loved one's passing often affect and stay with us long after their physical death. If our loved one suffered or experienced trauma, our memories can be all the more potent and challenging. We may replay their last moments on earth over and over in our mind, imagining the suffering or fear they might have experienced.

However, despite appearances, death can be so unlike what we expect it to be that when we pass over, we don't always fully recognize that this is what is happening. This is especially true when death is sudden or unexpected, particularly in accidents, traumatic events, and drug- or alcohol-related deaths. If we pass over after being kept physically alive with the help of medical equipment, or while undergoing surgery or other life-saving measures, we might also not recognize that we are leaving the physical world.

For instance, when Sarah, a middle-aged woman, came into my office, she was visibly nervous. Having never had a reading, she didn't know what to expect. As she silently sat across from me, she appeared to be trembling. Like others who have sat in that same chair, I knew that she longed to connect with a loved one.

When I began the reading, I felt a heavy sadness and felt that she was grieving a deep loss. I then felt the presence of a young, slim man with dark hair by her side. I described him to Sarah and asked, "Is this your son?"

"It sounds like him. My son passed over early last year. He has dark hair," she said.

"He's telling me that he didn't mean to die, didn't think that this would happen. He shows me that he was with friends, having fun, like a party atmosphere…It feels as if he had a problem with drugs and alcohol. Your son tells me that he liked the feeling of drifting away and relaxing…Now he shows me a man, gray hair and on the tall side, calls him Granddad. Your son says that he went with him. Everything felt light, he says, and he wants you to know he had no pain…"

A few tears rolled down Sarah's cheek. "I'm glad to know he is with my father. I felt that he might be. Is he okay?" she asked.

"Your son is saying that he didn't know that he died. He thought he was hallucinating when he saw your dad. He was trying to figure out how to get back into his body. I get the feeling from him that he still thought that he was high on drugs…He shows me that your father told him it was time to go and that they were going fishing, like they used to…Your son wants you to know that he felt and saw warm light and that it felt good, better than drugs…He says he wanted to say goodbye and your father guided him to your bedside…I see your son standing close to you; he wanted to be with you when you found out that he passed over."

"I don't understand. Are you saying that Jason didn't know that he died? How can that be? I would like to think that he didn't feel pain or suffer. It doesn't sound like he did. This gives me some peace," Sarah said.

"Your son's spirit left the body before he experienced the physical effects of a drug overdose. His soul recognized that he was passing over and, in its wisdom and love, released itself from the physical body. It doesn't hurt when we leave the body; there is no pain in passing. That is part of the physical experience but not the spiritual."

We Don't Suffer

In cases of severe trauma we are often haunted by images of our loved one's last moments on earth. From our human understanding we imagine what they may have felt or experienced before passing. Many who lose a loved one to unexpected trauma replay the shocking circumstances and live under the shadow of the stress and suffering this causes them.

This was true for Philip. When I began the session, he seemed skeptical and wary, and given his doubt I was surprised he scheduled a session with me. It was fairly obvious that he did not fully believe that I could communicate with the other side. However, when I described a woman with curly brown hair who told me that she was his wife, he became more interested.

"Your wife wants you to know that she didn't suffer," I began. "I believe she's describing her passing over. I see an image of a road at night and her lifting out of her body. She feels the sensation of warmth and light. Your wife wants you to know she wasn't alone. It looks like an angel, a light being, was there with her and also a small woman with white hair, possibly a grandmother. She says they protected her."

"How can you say she didn't feel pain," Philip interrupted me. "It was a horrible car crash. She hit a tree; the car was wrapped around it."

Although it had been over two years since his wife, Jennifer, passed, Philip still felt the sharp pain of suffering in his heart. The confusion, fear, and agony that he believed she must have experienced was almost too much for him to bear. He couldn't get the image of what he imagined her last moments on earth were like out of his head.

I saw Philip again about a year later. He had put on a little weight and looked better than he had the first time I saw him. The dark bags under his eyes were gone and he didn't appear to be as overwhelmed with grief.

He put his head down and said, "A few months after our first session, I was tired and fed up with everything. I was done trying to believe and act as if one day I would be able to move on and let go of the pain. I lay down on my couch and closed my eyes, hopeful that I would drift away into a deep, numbing sleep. Suddenly I felt my wife's presence. She was right next to me. It was so vivid; I felt the touch of her hand on my face. I knew I was dreaming, and I didn't want to ever wake up. I whispered, 'I love you, I love you,' over and over to her... At this point I was startled half awake, then suddenly I heard her voice. She told me that she loves me, but it wasn't just what she said. I could feel her warmth and happiness spread through me. I knew that she was okay and wants me to be too. She told me that she is close and that I've got to get on with my life here."

Like many others whose loved ones pass over in accidents or through other traumatic circumstances, Philip had a difficult time believing that his wife hadn't suffered pain and mental and emotional anguish. Yet, consistently, those on the other side report that they did not feel the kind of pain that we in the physical world would expect to feel. Instead, they describe the sensation of lifting or floating out of their body before an accident, heart attack, or other fatal physical event.

Once the spirit leaves the body, some describe watching the events unfold from a distance. In the company of angels and loved ones who have previously passed over, they feel no fear, only love. Several spirits have told me that they were not aware of the cause or manner of how they passed over. This occurs more often in unexpected and sudden deaths. Children go directly into a loving environment with the angels and loved ones on the other side and are shielded from the circumstances of how they passed over. Like all of those in the spirit realm, young people eventually fully transition into their ageless soul identity. From this heightened awareness they become aware of what transpired from a more enlightened soul perspective, free from anguish and suffering. People who have passed over suddenly or are not aware of the cause of their physical death also eventually become aware of the reasons for their passing.

What Is the Light?

When we pass over, we often speak of "the light." This is a common term that describes the emanating presence of all love, truth, and compassion. It is divine energy where all of our thoughts, actions, choices, and sense of self are embraced and healed. The loved ones who come to greet us when we pass over are a part of this energy and it radiates from them.

As we enter the light, we can never be sure who our welcoming committee will be. Often a parent, spouse, partner, grandparent, or child who we loved and knew well in the physical world greets us. However, I've had spirits tell their loved ones here in the physical world that a family member they didn't know well, or that they didn't know at all, helped them make their way into the light. Despite not knowing them in the physical world, their heart and soul immediately recognized these loving ancestors.

Sometimes a beloved dog or cat runs to us and happily guides us into the greater love. I had a spirit once tell me that a young deer came to her and led her into the light. As we pass out of the physical body, beings of light and angels are also present, sheltering us in loving warmth and comfort. Once we shed the physical body, our soul memory blossoms and we recognize our connection to other positive and loving souls, some of whom might not have been significant in our physical life.

Many religious people expect and hope to be in the company of the divine beings of their faith when they cross over. For instance, for Christians who believe in Jesus, Hindus who worship Krishna, and Muslims who love Mohammad, there may be a strong desire to encounter these holy beings on the other side. Many are often greeted by the divine presence in the form of their belief. For those of strong religious faith, seeing and being with Jesus or a particular saint is the joy of passing over. Many have lived their lives in such a way that they await the fulfillment of the heavenly paradise that their religion has promised. The heavens respond to our requests and wishes, and the power of our desire creates the reward that we expect.

Every so often in a session, a loved one on the other side excitedly lets my client know that they have encountered a holy presence. After losing her father, Krista, a busy mother of four, wanted a reading. After speaking to her father, I felt the presence of another spirit who seemed eager to come through.

"There is a woman coming in who has dark, shoulder-length hair. She's short, maybe five feet three inches or so," I said. "She shows me that she is from your mother's side of the family, an aunt, I believe."

"That's my aunt Anne. I was wondering if she was going to come through."

"She's here and she wants you to know that she saw Jesus, she went right to him. She says, she didn't stop to say hello to anyone else, she just wanted to see Jesus."

"That sounds like my aunt Anne. She was very religious," Krista said. "Can I ask her what it was like to see Jesus?"

"Your aunt tells me that Jesus is just as she expected him to be. She says that he is real and she's showing me that he welcomed her with open arms. She wants to be close to him, and I can feel waves of love coming from her to you. To everyone really, she wants to spread God's love to all that need it. Your aunt says to keep praying, and you don't have to go to church. She says, just love and pray to Jesus. I get the impression that she feels Jesus doesn't seem to care about our going to church but he responds to our prayers. They are important, she says."

Some who pass over feel unworthy or fearful of encountering a divine being. If we believe that we will receive retribution for our sins or that we didn't live a righteous life, we may be met by loved ones we are comfortable with. Slowly we realize that there is only love and no judgment and become aware of the divine presence within.

We eventually all become aware that the eternal and creative power from which all love emanates is greater and more expansive than one religion or understanding. The Divine can be found in all forms of worship and interpretation of God; it transcends and cannot be defined by one perspective. In this all-inclusive divinity we learn from different holy masters, seers, and teachers. There is no fear or restricting beliefs or practices that claim to have the "right" or "only" way. The atmosphere is one of all love and there is no dividing line between the divine and the mundane. We recognize the divinity within ourselves and become aware that our ultimate purpose is to embody and experience full surrender to this divine presence that is both within us and surrounding us.

Passing Through the Tunnel into Light

Our spiritual development here on planet Earth can prepare us for our passing. If we developed the ability to accept what comes our way in the physical life and let go of expectations, we have an easier time with our passing. When we cultivate a warm, open, and accepting heart, we can let go with more ease into the warmth of love and the arms of our loved ones who have already passed over. Even if we pass over during a traumatic event or debilitating illness, we are better able to trust the process.

Many who have had a near-death experience describe moving through a dark tunnel toward white light as their soul leaves the physical body. However, not everyone who has briefly visited the other side reports having seen or felt this phenomenon. This is also true for those with whom I have communicated on the other side. Not everyone has spoken of the presence of a tunnel. Some are quickly jolted out of the body unexpectedly and find themselves face-to-face with loved ones on the other side or in the presence of angels. Others quietly drift off while sleeping and peacefully wake in a heavenly garden, and some experience an awakening to a greater power and presence that seems to lift them out of the body.

However, there are others who describe in detail seeing a brilliant white light and the sensation of moving quickly through darkness toward this light in what appears to be a tunnel.

This is what happened with Ed, who was in his mid-seventies and had been sick for over a year.

When I gave a reading to his wife, Marsha, Ed quickly came forward with a lot to say. Friendly, warm, and loving, he was easy to communicate with and shared messages with his wife and for his children. When I asked Marsha if she had any questions for him, she told me that she wanted to know if he suffered during his illness and passed over in pain.

"I could never tell if Ed was in pain. He never wanted to upset me and always told me that everything was okay. When the doctor told him that there was a growth in his stomach, Ed told me that he wasn't surprised. For weeks he ignored the aching pain and told himself that maybe it was something he ate or perhaps he pulled a muscle mowing the lawn. It wasn't until he lost a bit of weight and started to sleep during the day that I insisted we go to the doctor. I tried to do everything I could think of to make him comfortable and ease his suffering, but he didn't want to cause me too much trouble. He had inoperable cancer and acted like everything was fine. One afternoon he called my son and let him know that he wouldn't be here much longer, but he never said a word to me. A few weeks later, we gathered around his bedside and he slipped away," Marsha said.

"Your husband is showing me an image of all of you standing around his bed. I can feel the warmth and love he felt from all of you. He shows me your faces fading and a glowing white light that peacefully surrounded him. The light appears to be in the shape of a tunnel, and I feel a buzzing vibration, almost like it pulled him into it. He tells me that he heard one of you tell him to go to the light."

"That was our daughter. She told her father this over and over. She felt he needed to be told what to look for."

"Your husband says that he listened and went toward the light. He shows me a woman whom I believe to be his mother coming toward him. She opened her arms and he effortlessly went to her. His death was peaceful, and he wants you to know it was painless."

The phenomenon of the light at the end of the tunnel is both a metaphor and an actual event. As a metaphor the tunnel represents our moving through the darkness of the physical life and its illusions and challenges into the clear light of truth and eternity. However, the tunnel is more than a metaphor and our imagination. As the soul prepares to depart, it detaches from the physical body. Without the light of the soul and spirit, the body becomes the dark tunnel through which the soul travels. The light is the emanating presence of all love and the divine presence guiding the soul to the other side.

While my mother was dying of cancer, she often talked about what she was experiencing. If she ever went through the stage of denial, it was short lived.

One afternoon after waking up from a nap, she told me how she felt pulled in two directions.

"My spirit wants to leave," she said. "It's pulling me up. I can feel it wanting to let go, but my body won't give up. It keeps pulling me back down. It doesn't want to give up either."

It was difficult to see her suffer in this way. She had no fear of death, but her body kept trying to keep her alive in this world despite her desire to pass over.

One morning, I woke up and knew that my mother was dying. I called my brother, whom she was living with, and he told me that she was peacefully sleeping. He didn't feel that her passing was imminent. Still I continued to feel the sensation of a vacuum-like suction force surrounding my mother that I had never before experienced. The intensity of this sensation was strong, and at some point I became aware that my mother's soul was moving out of her body and into the spirit realm. As I meditated and prayed for her, I intuitively saw her moving through what felt like a dark tunnel toward a brilliant light.

During readings, some on the other side describe this same kind of experience. They, too, report a buzzing, vacuum-like sensation and have the sense of moving through a dark tunnel toward the light. They feel no fear, just the blissful sensations of their spirit, which knows where it's going and what to do.

When We Don't Believe in Life After Death

Not everyone believes in life after death—that is, until we pass into the spirit realm and find that we are still very much alive. Those who didn't believe in God or a higher power, or who didn't give the idea of an afterlife too much thought while in the physical world, often go to sleep as they pass over in the belief that this is the end. The waking-up process can happen slowly or more quickly depending on the need of the individual soul. However, everyone eventually wakes up surprised that they still exist. While in this state of suspended conscious awareness, family and friends on the other side and compassionate spirits lovingly watch over them. Sleep also provides the opportunity for the energy body to rest and strengthen in preparation for an awakening into a realty that they didn't acknowledge or accept.

During sessions it is not unusual for someone who did not believe in life after death to come forward. For instance, Gemma, in her mid-thirties, was excited to see who would show up from the other side when we began our reading. When her grandfather Jerri came in she started to laugh.

"Ask him to admit that I was right," she said.

"Your grandfather says that like most things, you got this right too. Does this have something to do with his being in spirit? He keeps saying, 'Here I am, you're right.'"

"Yup, he thought death was the end. He didn't want to believe anything else," she said.

Not content to leave it at this, Gemma wanted to know if he was surprised when he found out that he didn't die.

"He shows me that he felt himself drift off, sure that this was the end. He says that he woke up and his father was sitting next to him. He says it was quite a surprise when he learned he had passed over. He still isn't sure how it all works. It's not what he thought, but he says he's glad to be alive."

If you have a loved one who is confronting their physical death, you can help them go into the sacred light of love where they will be cared for and re-join their family and friends. Talking with others about life after death can open a door for new understanding and acceptance. If you have a loved one who is in the active stage of dying, or if you have loved ones who are assisting another in passing over, approach the topic lightly and gently. Share your belief that there is life beyond the physical world and that there are loved ones on the other side who are waiting for them. If you are present with someone who is actively passing over or close to death, you could suggest that it may be helpful for them to go toward the warmth and light when they are ready to let go. Many loved ones on the other side have told me that they remembered the directions a loved one shared with them before they went over and they were helpful.

It can be difficult to watch someone we love in their last phase of life when death is imminent. If you are up to it, let your loved one know that you are available to listen if they would like to talk and share any of their concerns, fears, or stress about the dying process.

Above all, be sensitive to others' beliefs and their fears and frame of mind. Never overwhelm another with your beliefs and views or try to convince them. If it's not possible to meet them in their current beliefs, it is best to simply listen and pray for their peaceful transition and love them.

When We Miss a Loved One's Passing

Several years ago, I had a session with Diana. A couple of months after her father was diagnosed with cancer, Diana quit her job as an air traffic controller and moved to be closer to him. For almost a year she tended to his needs. She cooked for him, she took him to doctor appointments, and when he got too weak to do much, she sat at his bedside and read to him.

When his health further deteriorated, he was moved to the hospice unit at the hospital. When her father's death seemed imminent, Diana spent the night curled up in a chair next to him. The next morning, after listening to his labored breathing for several hours, she went to the bathroom to splash cold water on her face to wake herself up. A few minutes later she went back to his room and was met by a nurse who informed her that her father had just died.

More than anything her wish had been to be with her father when he passed over. Although she changed her life to do everything she could to make her father's remaining time easier, she felt that she had failed him.

When Diana came in for a session, she looked tired and sad. There was a shadow of a man behind her, and I knew that she was grieving his passing.

As soon as I began, the older man with kind eyes that came in with her began to talk.

"There is a man present and he tells me that he is your father," I said. After I described his appearance, particularly his kind eyes, Diana started to cry.

"Yes, that's my father," she said.

"He says that he is sorry; he's apologizing. There is something that he didn't give you."

"There was nothing my father didn't do for me or give me. He was a great father. I couldn't have asked for more," she said.

"Well, let me see if he'll explain this more," I said.

I sent her father a message letting him know that he was going to have to explain what he meant. I wondered if I hadn't read the message correctly. I waited and Diana's father sent me a stronger message. "Your father says that he didn't say goodbye. It feels that he passed over without you there," I said. "He wants you to forgive him."

"No, I'm the one who needs forgiveness. I went to the restroom when I knew that he was dying. I left him alone in his last moments. That's all I wanted, was to be with him, and I blew it," she said. "Can he forgive me?"

"Your father says that he knew that you left the room. His mother's spirit came close when you did, and he felt so happy to see her. Your father says that he had sensed that she was present for a while. When you left the room, he told her he was ready. He says he couldn't leave with you in the room. It was too difficult for him to say goodbye and to let go. He wants you to know this was his doing, not yours," I told Diana.

"Why? Why would he do this? I don't understand, I wanted to be there."

"He says it was too hard for him to leave you and hopes that someday you can forgive him," I said.

"Of course I forgive him," she said.

Over the course of my career I have had several clients who have experienced similar feelings of guilt for not being present when a loved one passed over. Situations like Diana's can be the most difficult. Even when we do all that we can to be present, we might still miss being there when a loved one makes their transition. On the way to be with a dying loved one, I have had clients miss planes, get stuck in traffic, get lost, or be told that a loved one has more time. A few clients have told me that their ill loved one asked them to leave or sent them on an errand, then passed over as soon as they were gone.

The power of love and our bond with a loved one can be so strong that it is difficult for a loved one to surrender and let go into the waiting arms of the eternal when we are present. However, it is not just loved ones that have a hard time letting go. Our fear of losing a loved one and releasing them to the great mystery of the unknown can act as a magnet pulling them back into the physical world. When the soul and body are ready to part ways, we need a clear path. It is often a relief and easier for our loved one to take flight when they are alone with spirit.

If you have a loved one who is making their departure from this world, give them permission to go.

Let your final gift to them be the freedom to pass over however and whenever they choose. Let them know it's okay to become spirit.

When We Get Lost

When I communicate with the other side, a loved one will sometimes come in who is not actually on the other side. When I describe who I'm communicating with, my client quickly lets me know that this "spirit" is still in the physical body. Every time this has happened, the spirit that I had been communicating with has Alzheimer's or some form of dementia and is very much still in the physical world. As Alzheimer's and dementia create fragmentation in the brain, an individual's consciousness often expands outside of the physical limitations and becomes aware of the spirit realm.

However, our spirit and consciousness doesn't go far from the body and usually alternates between being aware of and present simultaneously in both the physical and spirit realms. Sometimes the spirit can detach to the extent that it can visit loved ones already on the other side while still hovering close to the physical realm. However, all this coming and going can get confusing, and at times a soul may miss its own death. Adrift in the spirit realm, they are not sure why they are unable to reenter the physical realm and don't quite know where to go. Because consciousness is accustomed to going in and out of the body, the defining boundaries of the physical and spiritual blend together and some don't realize that they have died.

Something similar can happen when someone passes over as a result of alcohol or drug use. In an altered consciousness, the spirit detaches from the physical body and reality and drifts off into the ethers. If the body ceases functioning and dies, the spirit is not able to enter and doesn't know where to go.

Fear of death can also cause a spirit to resist going into the higher divine realms of the other side. Unfortunately, some people are afraid of what is going to happen to them after death. They may have grown up in religions that preach of a burning hell, or they are fearful of the devil or dark spirits that may lurk in the spirit realm. At times, this kind of fear can create a difficult and halted passing. As the spirit leaves the body it may resist ascending into higher spiritual vibrations and instead attempt to cling to something or someone still in the physical.

I've helped many wandering, lost souls make their way into the light, and it is not difficult to give them loving aid. Because lost souls still identify with the physical world, we are in the best position to help them. Although there are loved ones on the other side and angels who reach out to assist them, they are often unable to get their attention because the lost soul still clings to the physical perception.

If a loved one has not gone into the light, they need an energy source to stay in the physical world and will draw energy from their loved ones. They don't do this to hurt or scare us; they just don't know what else to do.

How to Help a Loved One Who Has Not Gone into the Light

Almost all of our loved ones go directly into the love and warm embrace of the spirit realm. Because it is unusual for a loved one not to go into the light, assume that they have. Rarely, a loved one passes over and gets confused, lost, or is afraid of going into the light. Those who believe that there is a God who will judge and condemn them may be fearful and cling to their loved ones in the physical world. Those who pass over as the result of an illness such as dementia, drug or alcohol abuse, or a sudden and unexpected passing might be confused and not see the light.

Common signs that a loved one has not gone over into the light are feelings of heaviness in your body, headaches, feeling very tired and worn out, or becoming ill. Other signs include hearing loud or subtle unexplained noises in your home, objects falling off of shelves, sounds of tapping or banging on the walls, or seeing or feeling dark shadows flying by you.

Through readings and personal experiences, I've encountered souls who needed a little help finding their way. For instance, a few days after a friend of the family committed suicide, I went into my office and saw her spirit sitting on my couch. She appeared to be patiently waiting for me. Surprised by her presence, I quickly realized that she was lost and had come to me for help. Instead of feeling white light, angels, or loved ones, the fog of depression and heaviness surrounded her. I sent her love and told her that she was no longer in her physical body and that her home was now in the light of the heavens. She seemed confused by this, as if she didn't know how to get there. I started to pray for her and asked Mother Mary and her angels to help guide her into the light.

Immediately I felt a humming, vacuum-type feeling and she was gone. Several weeks later, I felt her close. However, the heaviness and depression were gone. Instead, she felt light and peaceful, and I knew she had come to let me know that she was getting the help that she needed.

EXERCISE
Helping a Lost Soul into the Light

If you suspect or intuitively feel that a loved one has not gone into the light of the other side, try this:

- Say your loved one's name and tell them that they no longer are in the physical body. Explain as best you can that they have loved ones already on the other side who are waiting for them. You can send them this message through a thought or say this aloud.

- If your loved one has a parent or another loved one on the other side that they particularly trusted and were close to, ask for the presence of that loved one to help. If you are not sure whom to ask to help your loved one, ask for an angel or divine being to provide assistance.

- Send a message to your loved one that someone—another loved one who has already passed over, or an angel or divine being—is coming to help them and to be alert to their presence. Tell your lost loved one to follow the white light and warmth. You can send them this through a thought message or say it aloud.

- Pray for your loved one to be surrounded in love and protection, and ask the angels to lead them home. Prayer lifts our loved one's vibration and assists them in a smooth transition into the light. Our loved ones hear our thoughts like whispers and listen to our requests. Just telling them to "go to the light" provides them with direction. When we invoke the presence of divine love, God, or a higher power, it is immediately felt by those in spirit. Like parting clouds, the clear, brilliant light of the divine sends rays of love and comfort to those we love.

- Continue to pray and send love and white light energy to your loved one. At some point they will send you a message confirming that they are in the light.

Practices to Help a Loved One
Who Is Dying or Who Has Passed Over

Prayer and rituals can be helpful to a loved one who is in an active stage of passing over and for some time after they have departed. Many cultures and spiritual sects have specific practices to assist souls after passing into the afterlife. Most include such things as bathing the body and adorning it with flowers, incense, ash, or other scents and oils. The body might also be clothed in white or draped with special adornments. Some rituals include putting rice in the mouth and coins in the hand or placing favorite objects with the body for the soul to use during its journey into the light. In many cultures those who are mourning a loss might chant holy verses and recite prayers or special mantras to assist the soul in its ascension. These rituals and mourning activities can last for a day or two to a few weeks.

In our Western culture we don't generally attend to the soul once it leaves the body. However, even a small ritual or practice can help the departed soul into the higher vibrations of love. They also can help us to be closer to our loved one and grieve their passing.

Here are a few suggestions:

Prayer

Pray to whatever and whoever you believe in. This might be God, the goddess, a divine spirit, a higher power, or the universe.

The prayer can be as simple as asking and invoking this divine presence to guide and watch over your loved one as they make their journey into divine love and compassion. Don't forget to include yourself and other family and friends in your request for comfort and peace.

Visualization

Visualize the white light of love and protection surrounding your loved one as they make their way into spirit. This will help them even if they have been in spirit for several days or longer. Through intuitive soul awareness, they will know the white light has been sent from you and will feel closer to you. The warmth and love of white light will be a source of comfort. Along with white light, you can send a message to higher divine beings and loved ones who have previously passed over, asking them to watch over and guide your loved one.

Meditation

It can be helpful to become quiet, close your eyes, and open your heart. Although you might initially be overcome with grief, breathe and continue to open your heart and send love to your loved one who has passed over. Feel and accept the sadness and grief that will likely surface.

Eventually the emotional intensity will subside, and you will feel a sense of tranquility. In this stillness you may feel the presence of your loved one who has passed over. Continue to open your heart and send them love and allow yourself to feel the love they send to you.

Chanting

If you enjoy chanting or toning, this can be a good way to honor your loved ones. Sound is healing and carries love vibrations between the physical and spiritual realms. You might also want to listen to and meditate with chants or music used for sound healing. Open your heart and allow love to flow from you to your loved ones.

Even though we may have little reassuring physical-world evidence, know that any and all of your efforts to help your loved ones before and after they pass over are seen and known. Soon after being welcomed into the light, our loved ones begin the soul review. The next chapter provides deeper insight into this loving and enlightening process.

Chapter 2

The Soul Review

As we pass over, our awareness shifts from the physical and material to spirit, and we begin to realize that we are more than we thought ourselves to be. A perfect imprint of the physical self, our energy body appears similar to how we looked in the physical realm. However, in the high vibrations of the spirit realm, we appear younger, vibrant, and filled with light.

The journey of healing, restoration, and soul awareness begins as we leave the body behind. It is through the soul review, which usually occurs soon after passing, that the fundamental union between ourselves and the divine is celebrated.

As we enter into the soul review, we undergo a profound consciousness transformation. No longer ruled by the ego and limited thinking, we perceive ourselves through our soul's awareness. While we retain aspects of our personality and memories of our physical life, our perception of what we experienced is transformed. We become aware that the physical life offered us the opportunity to put into practice higher attributes of our true self, such as selflessness, forgiveness, and compassion. We recognize that what we created and the actions that we took here on earth either advanced or hindered our overall soul journey into the light of all love. When we put aside our self-centeredness, greed, fear, and negativity and choose the positive, we become aware of how our soul advanced. During the soul review, the love, kindness, and generosity of spirit that we have put into practice here in the physical world is a source of attainment and joy. The moments when we chose love instead of fear, brought hope to others who were in despair, and acted from the pureness of our heart, lift us into the higher vibrations of love and the wonders and beauty of the spirit realm.

Kenni Shares His Soul Review

Since passing over, Kenni, my ex-husband, has made it a habit to visit and share his experiences on the other side with me. Before we met, he had a successful career as a musician and songwriter. As a member of a few popular bands, he toured worldwide and played on national television shows such as *Saturday Night Live* and on MTV. At the height of his career, he was also writing and producing music for others.

After his father died, Kenni left New York and moved back to North Carolina to help his mother. That was when I met him. At the time, he was managing a music technology store and was only able to play and write music part-time. Three years after meeting, we married and he went back to playing and writing music full-time.

Although Kenni had always enjoyed a few drinks in the evening, his alcohol consumption increased after leaving his job. His work hours shifted to late nights, and he began to go out of town on a regular basis. Our daily routines and schedules were no longer in sync, and we would sometimes pass one another in the early morning. He would be coming home from a late-night gig and I would be heading out to work.

One day I came home from work and noticed him sitting on the couch staring into space. His eyes were dark, and he looked like a ghost of himself. In that moment I knew that he was using drugs. Although he denied it, in the coming weeks and months it was obvious that he had an addiction. The tension between us grew, and one day when our house became so thick with the dark and confusing energy that accompanies addiction, I told him I thought he had a problem and we needed to deal with it.

When I shared that I couldn't live with him if he was using drugs, he looked at me but said nothing. A few weeks later, while walking in the woods one early morning, I suddenly became aware that Kenni would rather end the marriage then stop using drugs and alcohol. It hit me like a ton of bricks. I still loved him, yet I knew there was nothing I could do to change the course he was on. Later that day, he asked me if we could talk and he told me that he was leaving.

Despite my request, he gave no reason for this decision and two weeks later we were living separately.

Now, he often comes to me from the other side and shares his experiences through images, thoughts, and feelings. He seems more willing and able to communicate now that he is no longer in body. Recently he described to me what he experienced shortly before his death and how it felt for his spirit to lift out of his body.

This is what he shared.

"As I got weaker, I began to see my mom and dad. (They are both on the other side.) I could feel them by my side; my dad's smile always relaxed me. Then one day they didn't leave. I didn't see them, but I knew they were close. I could feel their encouragement and Mom was telling me that it's gonna be okay. It felt so peaceful to be with them, I forgot about everything else. I just closed my eyes and...I must've been unconscious when I died, I don't really remember it. There was no stress or pain, just Mom and Dad with me, and I felt myself drifting into waves of color and light. It felt as if I was floating; there was light surrounding me and this pulsating soothing energy moving through me. I felt like I was part of God, like there was something very holy and loving with me.

"I was just chilling, happy to float along; then more intense energy moved through me. It was the oddest feeling. Like ripples of energy from within me bubbling up and surfacing as unexpected and intense emotions. I wanted to go back to just drifting and floating, but I couldn't stop what was happening. It was like a part of me knew what to do and I just did it. I felt someone close, like a presence, but I didn't know who it was. It felt good and loving, and it was stirring something up in me. I didn't hear any words and I just saw light, bright light...and felt kindness. Then I felt my mom and dad and others close; I just let go, I had no choice, and it felt good to let go. All of a sudden, I felt vulnerable and humble and allowed my heart to open and receive this overwhelming love.

"Then a big wave of energy bubbled up from within me and I began to see and feel memories from my life, starting with my childhood. These weren't just memories; I was experiencing past events in vivid detail and I knew and felt things that I wasn't aware of at the time. Some of the memories felt really good. I could feel the happiness and positivity that some felt when I played music.

When I saw myself play, it felt bigger than me, like something more powerful and joyful was moving through me. Then I had this awareness that it was never just me playing. I was part of something else, there was a powerful loving energy flowing from me, even though I never really was aware of it.

"Then other memories came that didn't feel so good. I didn't say or do things that I was proud of. The me that wasn't such a nice guy, that I was embarrassed by. Still I felt love and it was okay. This presence that was close sent me the message that I did the best I could at the time. It didn't seem to matter, what happened; I could just relax and allow love to flow through me.

"Eventually a bubble of energy moved through my heart and I felt your love for me. When you came into my life, it was such a gift. I felt your love and I felt my love for you and how happy and relieved I was to have you in my life. I thought everything was going to be good. Then I felt myself move away from you and harden my heart. I could feel how this felt to you, to be pushed away. I'm sorry. I wanted to relive my days of being free and I wanted to party and drink and do whatever I wanted when I wanted. I thought that you were in my way. I know now that it was just my immaturity getting the best of me and I hurt you. I got the feeling that part of why you came into my life was to help me grow up, but I didn't want the responsibility."

When Kenni expressed his awareness of the emotional impact that his choices and actions had on me, it had a profound effect. I felt his sincerity, and the pain and confusion of our breakup that was still lodged in my heart began to let go. It also got me thinking about how my choices and decisions might have brought him pain. For the next few days, my own memories surfaced. In one, Kenni was performing at an outdoor event. It was a warm and sunny day, and the crowd of people surrounding the stage was dancing and everyone looked as if they were having a good time. I stood on the side of the stage close to where Kenni was playing. When he glanced over at me with a big smile on his face, I rolled my eyes. I'm not sure why I did this, and I immediately regretted it. Kenni turned back to the crowd as if nothing happened.

As the memory surfaced, I felt the confusion he felt. It was a beautiful day made better by Kenni's music, and he felt belittled and uncomfortable by my unexplained behavior. I sent him an apology and let him know that I was proud of him that day for the joy he brought to so many, including me. A moment later, I felt his presence and warmth. His forgiveness seeped into my heart and I felt a little lighter and more open.

In the Company of Higher Beings

During sessions many of my clients want to know who greeted their loved one and what they experienced soon after passing over. Most of the time the question comes from my clients' fears that their loved one suffered and may have felt alone and scared. When someone passes over due to trauma, an accident, or an unexpected health issue, this is especially true.

Similar to Kenni's experience, many of my clients' loved ones on the other side report that they too had the sensation of floating upward into soothing and lighter waves of loving vibrations after passing over. After being welcomed by loved ones who have previously passed over, most become aware of higher beings. These higher beings stay close and guide our loved ones into the pure, peaceful, and loving vibrations of the soul review.

During readings, some have described what they believed to be angels, a loving presence, a wise master, or simply an embracing and warm light that felt holy. Others are not sure who or what is present, but they feel fully loved and known. Many communicate that they are in the presence of more than one being or a wise counsel or soul group. Often the spirit beings who come close after our passing have been with us during our physical life. They are advanced souls who have completed their earth lives and find joy in serving the greater good, one human at a time. In the physical life, we are rarely aware that there are loving beings watching over us and leading us to new awareness and opportunities. I've often thought that tending to us humans is likely a thankless and at times difficult role for enlightened beings. We tend to be strong-willed creatures who want our way and are often motivated by fear and selfishness. However, my guides assure me that they like and understand the challenge we provide, and they have a good sense of humor.

Along with our spirit guides we also have a guardian angel assigned to us at birth who is with us after passing over. Unlike a spirit guide, an angel has never experienced a physical life. They are pure aspects of God, divine spirit, holiness, or whatever or however you define the most loving and wise creative source of life. They are protectors of our inner divinity and keep us attuned to the love within and our higher aspirations. Without them life would be more difficult and challenging, and we could be plagued by utter hopelessness and a lack of purpose and joy.

The higher beings of light who come close and greet us after our passing are not strangers. Even though we may have never been consciously aware of them in the physical life, they are familiar to us. In their presence we feel a higher degree of love than we may have ever felt while on earth. The magnitude of their love, compassion, and kindness is humbling.

Along with spirit beings, many are aware of the presence of God, the goddess, Jesus, Mohammed, another divine master, or the higher power we believed in during our physical life. In this presence, some experience a holy transference of divine grace and forgiveness. Even for those who did not believe in a higher power, there is a sense of being in the presence of something powerful and good.

For instance, Catherine, a dark-haired young woman with multicolored tattoos covering most of her arms, seemed anxious when we began our session. Hesitantly, she asked me if I wanted to see the photos of her loved ones who had passed over that she wanted to connect with. I declined, telling her that I prefer to see who comes in on their own.

"If whoever you want to communicate with doesn't initially come in, we'll go from there," I said.

As we began the session, I became aware of an older, slim man who was wearing a cap standing next to her.

After I described him to Catherine, I said, "He wants to make sure that you know he has his cap on." As I said this, she relaxed in her chair.

"That's my grandpa; that's who I want to talk to," she said.

Catherine's grandfather talked at length and then gave messages for other members of her family. I then asked her if she had any questions for him.

"I want to know what it was like for him when he passed over. Did he make it okay?"

"I get the impression that soon after passing over he felt alone. Your grandfather is showing me an image of himself in a vast open space … Now he shows me a light; it is near him and as he wanders about, the light follows him. I feel fear, like your grandfather was afraid. Was he afraid of death? That's the impression I'm getting."

"Yes, he was. That's what I want to know. He didn't believe in God and was convinced that death was the end. His father was a preacher, and he rejected all of it. Grandpa grew up in a real fire-and-brimstone church where people believed in hell. I think he was always afraid that he was going to burn in hell and stopped believing in God."

"Your grandfather says that he wandered around for a while and didn't know where to go. This light being followed him, and he didn't know what to make of it…Now, he shows me an image of himself crying and he feels lost, almost like he's a little boy. He turns and he's talking to the light and asking for help…He says that he started to feel a tremendous amount of love and it felt as if his heart was going to burst. Then suddenly everything changed and he was in the light with his mother and other family members who had passed over long before him. When we fear that there is a God who will judge us, we might resist going into the light when we pass over. However, wherever we are there is love, forgiveness, and compassion. The divine presence is always with us."

"My grandpa took me in when I was a teenager. I was fighting with my mother and I went to live with him. He was always kind to me and accepted me just as I am. I just wanted to know he was okay," Catherine said.

"He's at peace in the light of love and still watching over you."

New Perceptions from Our Earth Life

Once we have encountered our loved ones on the other side and sense and feel the presence of higher beings, we are led into the higher vibrations of the soul review. Some on the other side have communicated that during the soul review they are alone or that there is a single angel or light being present. My spirit guides tell me that there are usually many divine guides, teachers, and loved ones present, but they don't want to overwhelm or draw attention to themselves and distract the soul from this important process. These beings assist and help us to balance the influx of emotions we experience by sending us waves of love and forgiveness.

During the soul review it is the beauty of our soul, along with wise and loving beings, that guides us. The manner through which the divine assists us is unlike the kind of help that the physical world offers. Here on earth we tend to be more aware of our ego's needs than the desires of our spirit. On the other side, we ascend into the wisdom of our soul and perceive our earth life through this enlightened lens. We have new insights and understand the deeper meaning and purpose of what we've experienced. Divine beings assist us in understanding our new sense of self and answer any questions we may have. However, they don't lecture, judge, or tell us what we could or should have done differently. Their emphasis is on loving us and encouraging our awareness of the divine intelligence within, which acts as a moral compass.

The soul review begins with what many have described as the appearance and sensation of orbs of energy that bubble up from within. In these orbs of energy, we view and simultaneously experience significant events from our earth life. As memories surface, they are accompanied by insights and new awareness into how our choices and decisions impacted our soul path. All that we do, think, feel, and experience in the physical life comes from the gift of free will and creative freedom. The root of this ability to choose and create lies in the masterful wisdom of the divine.

Through feeling our emotions and the emotions of those that we influenced and affected, we begin to more deeply understand and integrate our earth life experiences and lessons. As we continue to feel the emotional energy generated from our choices and actions, we are guided by powerful divine forces to come into a soul state of awareness. Soothing, peaceful waves of light energy flow through the energy body, opening the heart and allowing our true nature to emerge. There is no loneliness, selfishness, anger, frustration, pain, or anxiety on the other side. We are free to embrace our divine individuality and experience the joy that has always been within.

On the other side we don't process thoughts or struggle to understand. Instead of thinking, our awareness is intuitive and flows naturally from the core of our being, quickly and spontaneously.

Energetically woven within our energy body is a perfect record of our thoughts, emotions, and actions during our physical life. These memories that surface during the soul review do not come from our human thought or recollection. Instead, we experience them through soul knowing and emotion.

As bubbles of memories emerge, we become aware of those things that we judged as bad or felt shame and embarrassment about. However, through our enlightened awareness we are able to forgive ourselves and others, and we experience authentic compassion. Love comes to us from all directions, and we better understand the lessons within our life events.

We feel how our choices, words, and actions affected others, even those who may not have been directly impacted at the time. Not only do we feel how our actions affected others, we become the other and experience their reactions, emotions, and feelings as if they are our own. We feel the longing for love and forgiveness and the misunderstandings and contempt that we may have harbored about others and ourselves. Instead of recoiling and sinking back into an inner hiding place, our wounds call out to be acknowledged and healed. As our shame and embarrassment about past actions, beliefs, and thoughts are embraced by love, we are filled with peace. We realize that there is no judgment for anything that we experienced. It is all an essential part of being human.

Through an enlightened perspective, free of ego and self-centeredness, we are awakened to the soulful significance of our challenges, emotional patterns, suffering, and the unconscious pain and fear that motivated us. Instead of being a victim and feeling powerless, we perceive the many opportunities we had to share, give, express our gifts, and support and love ourselves and others. We realize that there was never anything to fear. Love was always close and we were safe. From this soulful perspective, we wonder why we took everything so seriously and didn't enjoy the beauty of the planet and others a little more.

During the soul review we learn that when we accepted our physical life circumstances and did our best to respond to whatever was asked of us in the most conscious and loving way that we could, we succeeded. The contrasts between the actions, thoughts, and beliefs that were motivated from our heart and soul and those that came from fear, human laziness, and ego are obvious. With help from divine beings and masters, we come to understand how the universe responds to and amplifies our intent, the positive as well as the negative. We recognize that when we listened to and acted on the dictates of our soul goodness, the universe responded by bringing us more positive opportunities. The love, forgiveness, and acceptance that we felt and expressed to others and ourselves in the physical world becomes a timeless source of joy.

There Is No Judgment

In some religious traditions, including Christianity, Islam, and Judaism, there is the belief that when someone passes over they go through a final judgment or reckoning by God. However, the soul review is not a time of judgment, retribution, or punishment.

Some believe that if you have committed what is considered a sin, the afterlife may be dismal. While those who lived a righteous life are in heaven, sinners are cast into hell. In ancient Egypt it was believed that a soul entered the underworld after death, where their heart was weighed on a scale of righteousness and truth. In Buddhism and Hinduism it is believed that our actions and decisions in the physical life become our karma. The sum total of our actions, both the negative and the positive, karma determines what we experience in the afterlife and in a future physical life. Karma can also be understood as the repetition of similar life lessons and circumstances from life to life.

When a loved one passes over, we may wonder where they are and what is happening to them. If we believe that our human character flaws and misdeeds are met with punishment and retribution on the other side, we may worry about our loved one's well-being when they pass over.

In the last several years I have had a marked increase in the number of readings I have done for mothers, fathers, and other loved ones who have lost a child or young person to drug or alcohol abuse or suicide. Their grief is understandably profound. To add to the immensity of their suffering, their religious beliefs may look upon their loved one's manner of death as a sin with the punishment of going to hell.

Many religions don't view psychics or communicating with the other side favorably. However, the desire to communicate with a loved one who has passed over motivates some conservative religious believers to seek out a session with me. Teresa was one of them. A petite woman with light blue eyes and a gentle smile, she sat quietly, waiting for me to begin. As I said a prayer, I became aware of her mother in spirit. She showed me that she often sat next to Teresa, holding her hand and sending her comfort. As she did this, I felt a wave of the loss and sadness that Teresa was feeling. Her mother then showed me a young man whose light blue eyes were similar to Teresa's.

"Do you have a son on the other side? Your mother is showing me a younger man; he looks like you," I said.

"That's Jason, my son. Is he all right? Where is he? I'm so afraid that he may have gone to hell. He was a good person, but my pastor and the people at my church tell me that he sinned. We all pray that he went to heaven," Teresa said.

"Your son is talking fast. I'll try to repeat what I hear... 'I was stubborn, it's not your fault... I feel the pain I caused you. I'm sorry, I wish I could take it from you...'" I said.

"I asked Jason to move out of the house before he passed over. My pastor told me he needed tough love and I had tried everything else," Teresa said. "Tell him to stop feeling my pain. I don't want my son to hurt anymore."

"Your son says that he is learning about his choices in life, but he feels only love... He says that he's getting help."

"Who is helping Jason? Is it my mother?" Teresa asked.

"He says he doesn't know their names... He says that there is a presence close to him, he can't see it like a person... more like a light... it's always with him... it feels good though. He doesn't feel judged or that it's mad at him or anything... He says that the light feels like love... it tells him that all, everything, is forgiven. Your son wants you to know that he's sorry; he didn't know how to change."

"Ask him if he's suffering. I don't want him to feel bad," Teresa said.

Jason was quiet for a moment than another stream of information came pouring in.

"He says it's not like that, he feels how he made others feel, but he also feels like it's okay too. He feels forgiveness and love at the same time. It's hard to understand... a part of him feels detached from it but aware of the pain at the same time. He says that he has memories of good times too. Like when he surprised you on Mother's Day when he was young and how his friends felt when he joked around... He didn't know he made people happy. This brings him joy. He doesn't know why he didn't know this. He says this light is always near him and talks to him and knows everything about him... it tells him that one of his gifts is lifting up others. Your son laughs and says that he kind of screwed that one up."

"Tell him that no one could put a smile on my face like he could," Teresa said.

"Jason can hear you and you can talk to him directly," I replied.

"Jason, I miss you so much. I miss your smile. Everything always seemed a little brighter and happier when you were there. I have to ask, could I have done something else to help you, something more? Did I do something wrong?"

"Jason says it's all on him... He knows it and it's the message this light sends to him. This was his lesson and challenge. He says he knows he had options and choices; you did all you could to help him. You tried. He says he didn't want to try. He was mad at life and wanted it to be different. He wants you to know that he can feel your love, and it feels so good, he floats in it."

"I have to ask him—did he want to die?" Teresa asked.

Jason was quiet. I could still feel his presence, but he seemed reluctant to answer. I asked him again.

"He says he doesn't know. He was confused but didn't think that the drugs would kill him. He kept taking more and more until his body couldn't handle it. He says that this light will help him figure it all out."

"What is the 'light'? Is that an angel or God or my mother or another relative helping him?" Teresa asked me.

"Soon after passing over we encounter light beings. Some describe them as angels or loving and wise beings who know the details of our lives and our soul purpose. Those on the other side often describe a warmth and light that emanates from these beings. It sounds like Jason is going through the soul review and becoming aware of how his actions influenced his soul plan and others," I said.

When I told her that the purpose of the soul review was increased awareness and healing and not judgment or punishment, Teresa relaxed a bit. The tension went out of her eyes and she seemed to be relieved that her son was not in hell. I explained that this is an opportunity to become aware of our choices and actions and evaluate them through the lens of our soul and heart. I let her know that loving, divine beings were caring for her son and holding him steady with love and that there is no fault finding, blame, or shame.

"People who pass over with addiction problems go to a kind of rehab in the sky where they are loved and well cared for. It is here among loving souls that they discover what led to the addiction and heal," I said.

Before we finished, I asked Teresa if she had any other questions.

"Would you ask Jason if he can help me? I don't know if I can make it here without him. I'm not sure I can go on."

I felt the presence of her son, but he didn't send any messages my way. Instead, he seemed to glow, and I could feel love welling up in his soul like a beam of intense light.

"Close your eyes," I said to Teresa. "I believe your son has a different kind of message for you."

As she did this, I saw the both of them wrapped in white light as one. A few minutes later, Teresa opened her eyes.

"I don't know how to put in words what just happened. It was like I was with Jason. I could feel the touch of his skin and his love, so much love. When he was born and I looked at his beautiful blue eyes, my heart opened. This is how it felt. He assured me that he would always be here for me and I believe him."

Acts of Love and Service Bring Peace

During the soul review we experience the joyful effects of the positive thoughts, feelings, and actions that we have contributed to others and ourselves in the physical life. In the business of everyday life here on planet Earth, so many of our difficult choices, random acts of kindness, and selfless giving go unrecognized. However, they are recorded and known in our spirit and in the heavens. It is often the small things that we say and do that are celebrated in the afterlife. Nothing is ignored or tossed aside.

Memories and experiences of giving to others, having compassion, and openhearted generosity are a source of joy and lift us into the higher vibrations of love. They also help us to better recognize and embrace our true self.

For instance, Ashley came in for a reading on a bright, sunny summer morning. Never having had a reading, she told me that she was nervous and didn't know what to expect. After I said a short prayer, I saw an image of a male spirit that felt like her father.

"Is your father on the other side? A slim, taller man with white hair comes in. It feels as if he had been ill before he went over," I said.

Ashley started to cry and said, "Yes, that's him."

"He is thanking you for taking care of him and says that he wasn't the easiest patient. He wants you to know that his passing over was easy; his mother came to him and helped him cross over. He tells me that everything happened just as you said it would. His passing was peaceful."

"I'm so glad to hear this—my father held on for a long time. It was hard seeing him so anxious."

"Your father says that he didn't want to leave. People were depending on him, and he seems concerned about others here in the physical world…I can feel his love for others…The angels are telling me that he helped and positively influenced many."

"He started a nonprofit and raised money to help feed and house the home-less. He gave so much of himself to others. I've wondered if this affected his health. He worked long hours, and when someone needed him, he was there," Ashley said. "He was kind and gave so much, always trying to do anything he could for those who suffered."

"Your father says that this is what made him happy. However, he didn't know if he was doing as much as he could. There were many who needed help that didn't get it…He says that now he knows that kindness and love matter. He says it's true that what you give to others comes back to you tenfold. Your father shows me an image of himself surrounded in light. He says that this light knows his efforts and intent and all the good he wanted to share and give. His heart and soul overflow with these blessings, and he feels deep joy. He is proud of you and of the work you do in giving and helping others and says that this is the true path to happiness."

Chapter 3

Variations of the Soul Review

We each pass over into the grace and love of the other side having experienced our individual challenges and circumstances. The soul review helps us better understand and accept the divine nature of our personal journey. No matter how difficult or confusing our lives may have been, the true value of what we experienced during our earth life emerges. Everyone's soul review speaks to their individuality.

For some, the soul review is an instantaneous process where we seem to know, feel, and experience all of our life in a momentary flash of spontaneous enlightened awareness. For others, the soul review can extend over a longer period of earth time. The emotional energy of some memories can be so intense and potent with new awareness and insights, we experience them in small increments. Those who were more aware and mindful of their personal growth and the influence and impact that their choices had on others during their physical life are able to move through the soul review with a bit more ease.

Those Who Knowingly Cause Others Pain

Our energy body or soul has an individualized vibration or frequency that is determined by our consciousness. When I tune in to the other side during readings, it is as if there are many floors where spirits reside. The spirit realm and all its inhabitants dwell in harmonious waves of light and vibrating energy. A lower floor or vibration is heavier and more dense. Spirits who knowingly caused others pain and suffering have a heavier vibration and reside on the lower levels. This is not purgatory and these souls are not suffering. Love surrounds and is within them and they are tended to by angels and loving beings. However, the non-loving actions, self-centeredness, and injury that they inflicted on others in the physical realm have to be felt and transformed through love.

The soul review for someone who knowingly inflicted pain on others is usually more drawn out and emotionally intense. As they sift through their actions and choices, these souls become aware of the effect they had on others and on their own evolutionary progress. As they feel the limiting patterns and the negative and painful emotions that they willfully created or fed into, they have the opportunity to develop empathy and compassion. During this process, the understanding that all actions come back to self and must be fully reconciled becomes clear. As the heart opens, the grip of fear, greed, and pain loosens. We become aware of how we allowed the harmful nature of our ego to keep us from truly loving ourselves and others. There is no judgment, and as we accept love, we experience peace.

Suicide, Addiction, or Self-Destructive Behavior

Souls who have taken their life through suicide or pass over as a result of addictions or self-destructive behavior reside in a sanctuary-type vibration on the other side. Devoted angels and divine masters lovingly watch over and help them to better understand their choices and actions while on earth.

When people take their life as a way to escape uncomfortable feelings, pressures, and the all-encompassing inner voice of depression, they are often surprised to discover that whatever prompted this decision must eventually be confronted and felt. On the other side there are no distractions, avoidance, denial, or running from the inner workings of the soul.

A soul who left the world through a drug or alcohol overdose or suicide rests in a warm, loving, and compassionate environment until they are able to proceed through the soul review. As they settle into a peaceful state, they often revert to a younger age prior to the addiction. As the soul review begins, they experience themselves at an age when life was less complicated and easier. Slowly they sift through and re-experience the choices and actions that led to their addiction, taking their life, or both.

The pain, anger, and grief that may have seemed so overwhelming in the physical life is slowly acknowledged and healed through the gentle embrace of self-love, compassion, and forgiveness. Some may try to resist the process of becoming aware and feeling the past. However, there is no rush and pressure on the other side to hurry or do more than a soul is willing to experience. The spirit realm is patient and there is no time. When a soul is resistant and slows down the soul review, they experience a kind of boredom and eventually move forward.

When I connect with those on the other side during readings, it is usually evident if they passed over as a result of suicide or an active addiction. Their freedom is somewhat limited, and although they can visit their loved ones on the other side, they are continually surrounded by angels in a healing vibration.

Those who take their life through suicide, self-destructive behavior, or an addiction that came about as the result of a mental or emotional illness or dysfunction experience a modified soul review. Soon after passing over, they find themselves with a loving, divine being in a healing sanctuary. As waves of divine healing energy move through their energy body, they are cleansed and purified, and they come into balance and mind, heart, and spirit wholeness.

Only the actions and choices made through a functioning mind and body are reviewed and experienced. Actions taken as a result of mental, emotional, or physical disease or ill functioning are quickly forgiven, better understood, and healed.

Traumatic and Unexpected Events

Those who have passed over through traumatic events, including such things as natural disasters, violence, or accidents, reside for a time in a peaceful and beautiful setting where they receive restorative care. Some souls who passed over through trauma are not aware of the events of their physical death and come to this awareness slowly as they become stronger and heal. During the soul review, they eventually become aware of how they passed but don't re-experience it in a difficult or painful way. Instead, they perceive it as part of a larger whole of their divine plan.

On a higher soul level, we agree to the experiences and challenges that we confront in our physical life. We don't do this to suffer or as a punishment. Difficulties can be a wake-up call for ourselves and for others. When we are not following the dictates of our soul, we may go over quickly and unexpectedly as a way to prevent ourselves from continuing on a path that is detrimental to our soul's purpose. I have had several spirits tell me that they were grateful for passing over, as they could not prevent or stop behavior or activities that they knew were not in their highest good. On the other side, they are able to make the kind of change that they were unable to in the physical life. This often happens when people have addiction issues or have gotten into a life of crime or other activity that is harmful to themselves or others.

Being Called to the Other Side

Some souls are called to the other side because they are needed for a specific purpose or to be of service. This is what happened to Peter. In the prime of his career as a researcher and physician, he was on the verge of a medical breakthrough into childhood leukemia. One sunny Monday morning he drove through a construction site and passed over when a steel beam fell on his car.

Peter's mother, Bonnie, is a petite, quiet woman who raised him and his sister as a single mother while working as a nurse. When she came in for a reading on the advice of some friends, she was visibly nervous. Soon into the reading, I became aware of a tall and lean man by her side.

"There is a male close to you; he has dark blond hair with a bit of a wave. He looks like you. Is your son on the other side?"

"Peter, it's Peter, my son," she said.

Peter talked about his childhood and shared detailed messages for his mother, sister, and wife.

Then he seemed to shift a bit and started showing me images that I couldn't fully understand.

"Your son is busy on the other side. He shows me what looks like some kind of scientific equipment. He seems to be engrossed in understanding something, even passionate about it."

"Peter was a scientist and very devoted to his work. Just before he passed over, a new grant came in that would have advanced his research," Bonnie said.

"Your son is telling me that he's still working on the other side. He says that this is why he passed over. He can do more to help others from the spirit realm than he could have down here. He says that he's working with other souls and that they make their discoveries and advancements available to others through the collective consciousness."

"I don't understand what that means. How can he still be doing his work and helping others?" Bonnie asked.

"Your son appears to still be working on medical advancements and helping others in the physical world. He says that when a scientist is ready and able to receive new information, it is sent to them from the spirit realm. Those in the physical world often receive the knowledge and awareness of what he and others in the spirit realm are working on through what can feel like an "aha" moment. Your son says he sends insights through intuitive whispers and transmitting thought messages. Of course, the recipients of this knowledge believe these ideas and insights come by way of their own thinking. Peter says that he didn't realize how much he was being aided by the other side until he passed over. He would still like to be here in the physical world but is finding peace through his continued involvement in helping others. He wants you to know that he couldn't have made the kind of advancements that he's involved in if he was still in the physical world."

Bonnie looked at me for a moment while trying to understand these messages from her son.

"My son's passing over didn't make any sense. He was such a good man, devoted to his wife and to his work. Everyone loved him, and he was doing so much good in the world. I don't understand all of this, but if he is able to help ill and sick children from the other side, I know he's happy. This gives me some peace. I'll still miss him though."

Souls that are called to the other side for service usually experience an uplifting soul review that highlights the purpose of their physical life and the impact that they had on others. As they experience their choices, thoughts, feelings, and actions, they feel the gratitude and love of all those that they helped. These profound expressions of love nurture, revitalize, and ignite their devotion as they continue to serve from the other side.

People might also pass over unexpectedly to help or wake up others in the physical life. These selfless souls have agreed before their birth to leave the earth in a way that will create positive change for others. The death of a loved one or acquaintance can have a powerful impact. I've had clients change careers, leave unhealthy relationships, go into recovery for addictions, and become a positive role model for others after losing a loved one. When a soul's passing is of benefit to others and an act of selfless love, they bask in the warmth of divine love during the soul review and move into a higher celestial vibration.

A Young Person's Soul Review

There is likely no greater grief than losing a child. It is difficult enough to let an adult loved one go. When a child passes over, the pain can feel unbearable. We miss their special smile, the light in their eyes, their laugh, and we grieve the loss of our shared future. We are biologically and spiritually hardwired to look after, love, and protect our children and do everything we can for them. When they pass over, our dreams, hopes, and a piece of our soul goes with them.

When we lose a child we are never the same; we essentially die to our old life. The door to the spirit realm opens and although we still live in the physical world, a piece of our heart and soul ascends with our child. Developing a spiritual consciousness that allows for communication with the other side has helped many of those who have lost a child. Through signs, messages, and thought or emotional intuitive communication, your child seeks to let you know that they are present and still with you. Although the grief will still likely be overwhelming and intense, developing the ability to become aware that our loved one is with us may bring a little relief to our suffering.

The soul review for a child varies depending on their age. Most young children who pass over haven't had the opportunity to make decisions and choices and have had limited life experiences. Their mental and emotional capacity has often not been fully developed, and opportunities to maturely exert their free will have been limited or nonexistent.

A child's soul review differs from someone who has had a longer earth life. Quite often it is an opportunity to relive positive experiences and become aware of how their life and passing affected others. The sly smile and warm hug that brought happiness to another, and their strength in the face of challenges, are more than small achievements. Through little acts of kindness, courage, and love, the soul advances.

Before we are born, we are aware of the challenges, opportunities, and the people that we are destined to meet. Most children who pass over at a young age come into the physical life for a specific purpose. Usually this has to do with providing a lesson or sharing a gift with their family and those they are close to. Children who leave the earth at a young age or during a pregnancy are special souls who often volunteer to come here for a short period of time to impact the lives of others in a meaningful way. Their passing may inspire another to value their life, to wake up to their gifts or deeper soul purpose, or to become of service to others in need.

When a child passes over, they still remember the spirit realm. They are going home and have no fear of life after life. Even though a child may have been young in physical years, the soul is ageless and timeless. As they reenter the spirit realm, children come into their full soul wisdom but may continue to experience themselves for a time in a childlike way.

As children age and further develop in the physical world, their ability to make decisions and choices increases, as does their free will and the ability to direct the course of their life. Adolescents and young people walk a thin line between childhood and adult life. When an adolescent passes over, their soul review is similar to that of an adult's. They become aware of and feel how the choices and actions they took affected and influenced others.

Quite often a short life span is part of a young person's purpose and it provides all that they have come here to experience. As difficult as it is for us here on earth to lose a young person, the soul has no age and doesn't measure the significance of physical life by time. However, for the family left behind, this doesn't necessarily make it any easier.

After a young person passes over, their family and friends must navigate through unknown terrain. Nothing has prepared them for the deep, raw cut in their soul that occurs when a child goes into spirit. Life is forever altered. Catapulted into a new reality, those left behind often feel as if they are someplace between heaven and earth, and neither one may feel like home. The friends and family of a child or adolescent who has passed grieve not only for the loss of their loved one but for the life they didn't have the opportunity to live and experience.

A Full Life May Be Short in Years

My clients who have lost children often feel as if their own life has ended. They don't know how to move forward and are not sure they want to. Often there are regrets and recriminations as to what they could have done differently. The haunting thought that they did not fulfill their purpose as a parent and that they somehow failed their child often covers them like a shroud.

Karen contacted me for a reading on the recommendation of a friend. As soon as she and her husband, Steve, came in my door, it was clear that they had suffered a tremendous loss. Underneath the polite and kind demeanor, I felt their pain and saw deep sadness in Karen's eyes. She had never had a reading, and I could feel the importance of our session.

Once we began, I felt the other side open up, almost in a grand welcoming gesture. There were souls who had been waiting for this opportunity, and like Karen and Steve, they were ready to get started. After connecting with Karen's grandmother for a few minutes, an energetic, smiling, and dynamic adolescent male came through. He had wavy blond hair and blue eyes. As I described him, I realized that this was their son.

"Your son wants you to know that he's found what he's good at. He's helping others, young people still in the physical world who he says are like him. He says that he sends them positive thoughts and does his best to help kids who are struggling and feel alone. There are other spirits who are guiding him in this work. It seems important to him that you know that he is doing this, that he's found his purpose," I said.

I looked over at Karen and Steve and they both sat motionless and didn't say anything. Their son continued to talk and share more messages for his parents and brother. However, he kept winding back to his purpose.

"Again, your son is telling me that he couldn't find what he was searching for here. He says he was lost and didn't know what kind of career or work to pursue. I get the impression he liked the outdoors and spent a lot of time in nature. He shows me that this is where he felt calm and peaceful. The world was a maze for him, and he didn't know where he fit in."

"We didn't know how to help him; we tried so many things. He became increasingly frustrated and confused as he got older. He had been such a happy and outgoing kid. Everyone loved him, but this started to change as he got older," Karen said.

"It feels as if your son passed over as the result of an illness. He wants you to know that he's feeling good, really good, and full of energy. He's not confused. The illness must have affected his thoughts or thinking. He points to his head and says that everything is clear now."

"He died of a brain tumor, a fast-growing inoperable one. He passed over less than a year after being diagnosed. It was too early; he was too young," Karen said.

"Your son says that he lived his full life and he is where he is supposed to be. He understands now why he couldn't figure his future out and had no desire to plan or think about it."

I looked at Karen and Steve and noticed the puzzled look on their faces.

"My son was always so healthy and full of life. Why was his life cut short? I don't understand, he had so much to look forward to—we all did," Karen said.

"One of my guides is coming forward and wants you to know that your son lived his life plan. Life here, as you know, is not always easy. We have to figure a lot of things out, such as what makes us happy, how to make a living, and what our contribution will be. We have to make money, pay bills, and make choices that impact ourselves and others. Your son didn't come into this world for these challenges. His purpose was to experience a carefree young life, be close to the natural world, and have a sense of freedom. You both gave this to him. His childhood was stress free and he was able to explore the wonders of nature through the eyes of innocence. You gave him this incredible gift and fulfilled your purpose as his parents. He was, and still is, being loved by you both exactly for who he is."

I looked over at Karen and Steve, who were listening to me with focused attention.

"As your son got older, he experienced and learned more about the angst and challenges that young people go through. I'm told that his purpose on the other side is to help young people. He's becoming a spirit guide to those in the physical world who are struggling with the same issues that he experienced."

Karen and Steve both asked a few more questions and then quietly left. I felt their son's spirit follow them out the door and into the car, still doing his best to comfort them.

An adolescent's soul review provides insights into the purpose and lessons of their physical life and is a loving experience. When an illness or physiological issue has affected an individual's clarity of heart, mind, and soul there is instantaneous healing and peace. However, even when our choices and actions were made through a sound self-will and mind, we are not judged or condemned. As we feel the emotional impact that our behaviors had on ourselves and others, we experience the healing power of compassion.

Beginning the Soul Review Before Passing Over

Those who pass over due to a debilitating long-term illness, or mental or emotional dysfunction, often rest in a peaceful, loving environment in the company of healing light beings. Once the physical body is shed, there is no pain, suffering, or discomfort. Those who may have suffered with dementia or Alzheimer's are no longer confused or disoriented; their awareness is clear and lucid. After a long-term illness, the soul may rest and rejuvenate the energy body through the warmth of love. During this rest period, healing angels and loved ones who have previously passed over visit and watch over them.

Some who suffer from long-term illness begin their soul review while they are still in the physical body. While they are sleeping or in a semiconscious state, memories may surface. As they recall past conditions and experiences, they receive new awareness and insights about how their choices and actions may have affected others. Seldom, however, does this feel out of the ordinary or unusual. Some who begin the soul review before passing over have the opportunity to ask for forgiveness or share heartfelt and authentic feelings with those still in the physical world. When the soul review begins before passing over, angels and divine beings are still present, silently guiding and supporting the process.

When someone passes over after a long-term illness, or with Alzheimer's or dementia, the soul review enables them to gain insight into the soul lessons or circumstances that triggered their illness. When it comes to our soul, everything that we experience has meaning and purpose. Our soul may elect to use illness as a means through which to learn and practice such things as how to be vulnerable, how to allow and trust others to care for us, and how to love ourselves. Illness also gives us the opportunity to transform before passing over. It is always preferable to evolve and practice self-love while we are in the physical life. That is, after all, what we have come here to do.

During the last year of my mother's life, she suffered with cancer that had spread throughout her body. She didn't want to receive chemotherapy or any other treatment and would have been happier had she passed over when she was diagnosed. Day by day the cancer ate away at her, and she slowly became a shell of who she had been. She knew she was dying and was unhappy that she was alive.

Watching her suffer knowing that the outcome would be physical death was difficult. After she passed over, I asked my guides if there was a reason or purpose in such suffering. It seemed so senseless and cruel. Their answer came quickly.

"Her slow passing gave her the opportunity to examine her life," they said. "This was an opportunity for increased awareness and to still make evolutionary soul progress while in body."

In her physical life, my mother was angry and self-centered. As she got older, she became increasingly resentful that she didn't have an easier life. She was a physically and emotionally abusive parent who didn't express remorse or guilt for the suffering she brought to me and my siblings. A few weeks before she passed over, she called me late one night crying.

"I'm sorry," she said. "I've been a bad mother. Would you forgive me?"

Considering she lived her life in complete denial of the pain she inflicted, her admission was unexpected and almost miraculous. The hours she spent confronting her passing made a difference, and I forgave her.

When I asked my spirit guides about her surprising admission, they told me that illness can be a way to release negativity. Our suffering can become an active type of karma that allows us to discharge the negative energy that we have accumulated and transform it before we pass over. In this way, we more quickly move into a spiritually-higher vibration of love and joy after passing. For some, the depth of awareness and transformation can be so profound it leads to physical healing and recovery. We don't become sick because we are bad or are paying for our negativity or something we have done. Transforming our emotional pain, and developing compassion and forgiveness, allows positive energy and love to flow through us, which may result in spontaneous physical, emotional, and spiritual healing.

A Grandmother's Love from the Other Side

During the soul review, we come into vibrational alignment with our true self and soul energy. The higher our vibration, the more freedom, creative activity, and joy we experience. Our vibration or consciousness is determined in part by the evolutionary soul progress that we attained in the physical life. The soul review magnifies the kindness, love, and compassion that we expressed in the physical world and is a source of joy.

As we rise into higher vibrations on the other side, our soul is restored, and we experience the bliss of creation. Souls who inhabit lofty, heightened vibrations often describe the environment as one of incomparable beauty. The skies are more lush, colorful, and vibrant than anything on earth. Many speak of gardens where the flowers, streams, animals, and vegetation are alive and seem to lovingly reach out and speak to them. If you have ever wondered where the souls of your pets go when they pass over, it is often in these higher vibrations where they, too, experience peace and rest. Some souls describe being in the presence of divine and holy beings and the enlightened wisdom that they share.

Loved ones who reside in higher spiritual vibrations can provide a positive influence on our lives, bringing abundance, positive opportunities, and healing our way.

For instance, I had just started the reading with Randa when a small and quiet woman with white curly hair came forward from the spirit realm.

I described her to Randa and told her that it felt like this was her grandmother on her mother's side.

"Your grandmother is proud of you. She says that you've made it and you're stronger every day. I get the impression you were sick. Your grandmother shows me what looks like a hospital. You must have gone through a lot of tests and treatment. Your grandmother says she's tried to help and comfort you in any way she can."

"Oh, I believe she has been with me. On one of my worst days, when my prognosis was not good, I felt her by my side. I smelled her perfume and it felt as if she put her arm around me," Randa said.

"Your grandmother wants you to know she's never far away and that you're going to be okay. She's been praying for you and sending you healing."

As Randa wiped away a few tears she said, "At one point my doctor told me that my cancer wasn't responding to treatment. It didn't look good. I knew there wasn't much more they could do. I thought my life was over. I didn't have the will to go on. I was so tired and drained from fighting the illness. That night I woke up and it felt as if my grandmother was by my side. I felt and heard her whisper in my ear. It was kind of amazing. The hairs on my arm stood up and I suddenly knew that everything would be all right. Nothing could shake that feeling, it was so strong. A few days later, I started a new type of treatment. Even though it was experimental, it worked right away. No one could quite believe it, but I did. I knew it would. My granny told me so. I think she helped make it happen."

"Your grandmother certainly is determined and loving. She says that you're her angel and she will always be close."

"She always called me her angel… My grandmother worked hard all of her life; she raised her sister's children and worked in a mill but never complained. Is she resting now and at peace?"

"Your grandmother shows me an image of a garden; it's full of roses and daisies and fruit trees. The sky is lit with shades of magenta and gold. Your grandmother is relaxing here and at peace."

"She always loved her roses and peach trees," Randa said.

Although our conversation was similar to many other medium sessions, the kindness and love I felt in the presence of her grandmother felt extraordinary. Her family and friends in the physical life were blessed to have her.

The soul review heals and transforms our loved ones on the other side, and it helps us to heal as well. The emotional burdens, worries, and confusion that our loved ones may have experienced in the physical world fall away. They perceive through clear eyes of soulful love and rest in the harmony of celestial peace. This energy flows to us as our loved ones come close to share their love. In the next chapter we'll explore what our loved ones experience after the soul review.

Chapter 4

The Infinite Possibilities
of the Other Side

L ife on the other side, with its infinite possibilities, is a mystery. We often
think of the other side as a place that is far away. We've never seen the
other side through our telescopes, and our astronauts have never landed in the
place where our loved ones go. To understand the other side, it's important to
remember that it is not so much a tangible location as it is a vibration. Like a
two-sided coin, night and day, or the yin and yang symbol, the physical and
spiritual worlds are connected and complement one another.

As we move through the soul review, we become increasingly aware of
the peace and beauty of the spirit realm. As the burdens of the earth life are
released, our spirit environment comes into greater focus. Some I have communicated with on the other side describe and show me images of ethereal
panoramas similar to the physical earth's sunrise or sunset but more colorful,
sublime, and peaceful. Others speak of being in forests, near rivers or streams,
or on the top of a mountain, gazing out at indescribable beauty. Many spirits talk of traveling to the locations that they had always wanted to visit while
in the physical realm. I have had those on the other side tell me that they are
climbing mountains, visiting exotic locations, and enjoying themselves on
cruises.

The earth that those on the other side visit is indeed our physical earth.
However, they experience it in a more pristine and pure state, where there is
no pollution, crime, suffering, or disharmony. The spiritual earth vibrates at a

higher nonphysical rate, coexisting with the physical earth—but, like our loved ones, it exists in another dimension.

Those on the other side perceive the current physical earth activity through a kind of film or mist. They may be able to see us, feel our feelings, know our thoughts, and sometimes intuit the future. However, not every spirit is able to clearly perceive everything happening on the earth and with their loved ones. I've had clients ask me if those on the other side are able to see and know when they do such things as take a shower, pick their nose, or fumble about in a variety of awkward or embarrassing situations. Don't worry, our loved ones are generally not aware of these kinds of activities and have no interest in them. No one on the other side can come close and watch us if we don't want them to. What gets their attention and amplifies their ability to tune in to us is our emotional energy and our thoughts. If you are going through an experience that stirs up your emotions, both positive and not so positive, it is easier for those on the other side to be aware of you. However, if you want to be alone or are involved in an intimate act, they are aware of your desire for privacy and cannot intrude.

Exploring Different Time Periods

Some spirits are able to experience the earth in different time periods. In the spirit realm there is no linear time; instead, everything is happening in the now. However, past earth events can be experienced through entering into other dimensions. It's almost like walking into a movie theater, except it's not just an auditory and visual experience. When we enter into another time period, we experience the intensity, feelings, and thoughts of that time.

Not all spirits are able to access these various levels of reality. Again, it depends on our level of consciousness. When our consciousness and vibration is more highly evolved, we experience more freedom and choices. However, this isn't a reward or treat. Instead, increased awareness opens doors to more creative exploration and freedom. When we have been able to love ourselves and others through the pure love from our heart and soul in the physical world, we move into the spirit realm with a higher consciousness and vibration.

During and after the soul review, some explore past events and the soul's journey through other lives. This can aid us in better understanding the origin of the repetitive patterns and difficulties they encountered in the physical life.

Sometimes the interest in past civilizations and other times answers questions and gives insight into the magnitude of our soul's wisdom.

Years ago I did a reading for Carrie, a young woman who worked for the city as an engineer. When I began the session, I felt the presence of a male who felt like her father. I described him as a tall, thicker-built man with hands that had the rugged look of someone who had worked outdoors.

"That would be my father; he was an electrical lineman. I was hoping that he would come in," Carrie said.

"He's with you quite a bit and sends you signs through birds. It looks like hawks and owls. Have you heard an owl outside your bedroom window in the morning? He laughs and says that he's your alarm clock."

"Just this morning an owl woke me up," she said.

Carrie's father continued to share messages, and when I asked her if she had any questions for him, she asked, "What's he doing? Is he happy?"

"Your father is showing me an image of what looks like a scene from a long time ago. It looks like he's in a vast expanse surrounded by pyramids, like the ones you would see in Egypt. Only this scene is not present time. There's a lot of activity. It looks like it might be during the time when the pyramids were being built. I asked your father about this and he says that he's so happy to finally be getting answers to his questions."

I was a bit perplexed by what he was showing me and thought I wasn't getting his message right. So I asked Carrie, "Does this make any sense to you?"

"Several years ago, he and my mother traveled to Egypt to the pyramids with a tour group. After that he read whatever he could find that would give him insight into how and why the pyramids were built. He became a bit obsessed with it. I'm glad he's getting his questions answered. I'm not sure how this all works, but I bet he loves being able to learn about it."

"Your father says that he is learning about how the pyramids were built, but there are other things he's learning too. He says that he always wondered why he had a fascination for the odd and unusual and always felt a little odd himself. He says that before humans as we know it walked the earth, there were a variety of different life forms from other star systems and galaxies who toyed with inhabiting the earth. He says that he was one of the otherworldly life forms that came here to check it out," I said.

Before I could finish, Carrie interrupted me. "That sounds just like my father. He loved science fiction and researched extraterrestrial life and anything unusual. I'm glad he's indulging himself and getting the answers he's always wanted."

Carrie then changed the topic, and I was never sure if she believed what her father said or not.

Socializing

After many years of communicating with souls who have passed over, I'm still surprised and somewhat mystified by what those on the other side tell me about the afterlife. Just as we have free will in the physical world, we have the opportunity to create our experiences and steer our evolution and growth in the spirit realm as well.

After the soul review, many stay close to family members on the other side. They may recreate much of how they lived in the physical world. Some have described dwelling in a childhood home or another favorite place. However, they are not inhabiting an earthly space, but recreating this experience in the spirit realm. Many continue to enjoy many of their favorite earth-life activities. I have had those on the other side share that they are doing such things as playing cards, fishing, or painting.

People who have passed over before they had the opportunity to enjoy retirement often engage in the things they had hoped one day to do in the physical world. They might sit by the lake and fish, learn a new creative hobby, or just relax. Many love to socialize and go to parties.

I did a reading not long ago for Kristin, whose mother passed a few years prior to our session. After Kristin moved into her mother's home to take care of her after she was diagnosed with late-stage cancer, she stayed with her night and day until her mother peacefully passed over.

Excited to communicate with her, Kristin was surprised when her mother did not come forward at the beginning of our session. It wasn't until about halfway through our time together that I sensed her presence and described her blond hair and slim stature to Kristin.

"Yup, that sounds like Mom," she said.

However, when I told Kristin that her mother was wearing a bright red dress, she seemed confused.

"I don't remember my mom ever wearing a red dress. She typically didn't wear dresses—more of a polyester slacks kind of woman," Kristin said.

"Well, she's wearing a dress now, and she wants you to know she's enjoying herself. Your mom shows me an image of her salsa dancing."

"She could barely walk the last few years of her life—had a hip injury and painful arthritis. I guess she's making up for lost time… She did love dancing when she was younger. It makes me happy to think that she's back at it," Kristin said.

Visiting Friends and Family Here and on the Other Side

Our family and friends on the other side are often in the company of their loved ones who have previously passed over. In addition to socializing and having fun, they mend unhealed past issues and discover new aspects of one another's individuality that they might not have been aware of in the physical life. Even relationships in the physical world that may have been short lived and seemed less significant, like those we had with a neighbor or a coworker, are often revisited.

We may encounter our past loves and those that we had always wanted to meet. However, we don't seek out those who were popular, rich, or famous while in the physical world simply to be in their company. There is no ego on the other side, so our desire to be with others is based on authenticity and shared consciousness. Whatever fame or worldly achievements we might have enjoyed in the physical world are only as valuable on the other side as the love they expressed and the good they did for self and others. The worldly rich and famous are simply souls just like us who have their own life experiences and evolution to guide them.

Most of those on the other side also like to visit and be close to their loved ones in the physical realm. Love draws us to one another, and our loved ones are never far from us. We tend to think of visiting family and friends in the physical world in terms of distance and the amount of time it takes to get from one place to another. However, space on the other side is defined more by intent, love, and soul connection. When we love another and have the intent to be with him or her, we are instantly present.

During readings, those on the other side often describe their loved ones' homes in detail. They may mention that they like sitting in the tan recliner near the fireplace or playing with the clock in the hallway. I had a client once who couldn't quite accept that I was able to communicate with the other side. So when I told her that her mother was often in her home quite a bit, she scoffed at the suggestion.

"How do I know that this is really my mother?" she asked.

"Well, she doesn't have your blond hair. She comes through with short, dark hair with a little wave in it. She's petite with a slight build," I said.

"That sounds like her. How do I know that she's in my house?"

"Your mom shows me a couch cushion; it appears to be light blue-gray. She keeps turning it over. I'm not sure why. Did you stain one of your cushions and turn it over to hide the stain? That's what it looks like she's doing."

"How would she know that … This is a little scary. No one knows that I did this. I recently spilled red wine on the cushion and couldn't get it out, so I just turned it over."

Our loved ones especially like sitting outdoors on our patios, decks, or in our backyard. They might send birds or squirrels to the window to get our attention to let us know that they are present. They enjoy being in our company and peacefully sit by our side. After a stressful day or when problems feel overwhelming, they offer quiet comfort.

Loved ones on the other side also enjoy riding along with us in our cars. I had a client named Brenda whose grandmother told her that she loved to quietly sit in the passenger seat while she drove. She listened to music along with her and sent her love and comfort. Brenda's work took her all over the state day after day, and she loved the thought of her beloved grandmother being by her side. Many of our intuitive conversations with our loved ones occur while we are driving or doing such mundane things as folding the laundry or cleaning the bathroom. Much of the time we aren't aware of their presence, and it feels as if we are wrapped up in our own thoughts. However, those little insights and awarenesses we receive when alone might be coming from a loved one on the other side.

The Young in Spirit

Children and young people who pass over after a period of suffering or neglect go to loving havens where their spirit is restored and strengthened. Often these environments are soothing, beautiful gardens with glistening pools of healing water, blooming flowers that speak of love and gentle healing, and animals that roam about. These gardens are inhabited by angels and loving souls who heal and care for these newly arrived souls. Loved ones and family who have already passed over visit and watch over the young. Even if they had already made their transition from the physical world to the spiritual before the child was born, they lovingly attend to them. From the earthly perspective, we are rarely aware of those who love us from the other side. However, when we pass over our soul recognizes those who have been close by, and we feel an instant connection.

From this safe haven, young people who have passed over journey to the family in the physical world that they left behind. Although the presence of these young souls is not always detected, their influence can be a source of comfort and support to their family during the grieving process. After the soul review, the young may continue to learn and grow through the lessons they were experiencing in the physical life.

For instance, I've worked with many parents who have lost children in their late teens and early twenties. This is a time of transition from youth to adult responsibilities and maturity, and not an easy passage for many to navigate. Those who pass over at this critical juncture continue to learn more about why they faced the challenges they confronted in the physical life. Becoming aware of the significance of our choices is especially important when alcohol, drugs, suicide, or risky behavior leads to passing over.

After the soul review and rejuvenation and healing in the gardens, those who pass over in their youth join with other souls. The young don't stay children for long on the other side, as the soul is eternal and has no age.

Some of the young people who come through in sessions talk of attending school-like environments where they are among other souls learning similar lessons. They may study such things as creativity, love, universal laws, and how to influence and contact those in the physical world. Many learn more about their soul's journey through different lives and become aware of how to better express their soul's individualized contribution to the greater whole.

Those who seek to be of service and help others still on earth learn more about the history and evolution of physical life and explore different spiritual traditions and intellectual and philosophical movements. They become aware of the gifts that they have cultivated and how to best express and share them.

Children who pass over come to the earth life for specific reasons and purposes. Sometimes they need to experience being part of a family or a specific age or developmental level. At times a soul chooses to incarnate to experience limitations in order to make rapid soul advancement. This might involve living a short life with an illness, handicap, or other condition. Even though it appears that the suffering that some soulfully consent to is without reason and senseless, the soul always has a purpose. Most of those who pass over when young have come to the physical life to teach, create new awareness, and bring change and transformation into the lives of others.

Although the children who pass over will always be someone's child, sibling, friend, or family member, they continue to evolve and come into their full soul self on the other side. Their activities and continued evolution and growth are determined by their consciousness level and not by the age they were when they passed over. Many who are here for a brief time are highly-evolved, old souls who quickly advance to creative and influential levels of activity and service to others.

There is no limit to what our loved ones on the other side are creating and experiencing. The soul longs to come into full expression and leads our loved ones deeper into their individualized evolutionary process.

We are forever in movement, evolving, expanding, and growing in both the physical and spiritual realms. In the next chapter you'll discover more about soul groups and service opportunities in the spirit realm.

Chapter 5
Soul Groups, Service, and Purpose on the Other Side

Several years ago, I noticed that the information loved ones expressed to my clients was beginning to evolve and deepen. Those on the other side started to share such things as how they were involved in altruistic group projects, and some spoke of being part of larger-scale efforts to solve some of our earthly issues and problems. A few shared their adventures and explorations to other galaxies and star systems. When I asked my guides for help in understanding some of what I was receiving, they explained to me that as we evolve and expand, we experience unlimited creative possibilities. In these new experiences we soon realize that it is when we seek to uplift and support others that we feel the most joy.

As we settle into our new lives on the other side, we often recreate much of what we experienced in the physical world. We might live in a similar home among our loved ones who have previously passed over or take part in the same pastimes and hobbies. However, before long a curious and unexpected shift takes place. We become a bit bored and begin to wake and realize that there is more to us than what we thought. New aspects of our greater being, our soul self, begin to emerge.

Depending on our level of consciousness, this awakening to our greater self can be subtle or, at times, more dramatic. Remember, our level of consciousness is determined by the degree to which we have been able to integrate our soul, truth, and love into our conscious self during our earth lives. Our soul is always on a journey to expressing the higher truths of forgiveness, unconditional love, service to others, compassion, selflessness, and generosity. As we integrate these attributes into our physical and spiritual self, we raise our consciousness and vibration. Our earth lives are essential: we take what we have learned to the other side to further expand our experience of who we are. The higher our consciousness, the easier and more natural it feels to accept and flow into our greater potential and wholeness.

Although we often attempt to recreate our earth experience on the other side, the divine force counters this desire and continues to call to us. It stirs our heart and soul with the warm breeze of freedom and invites us into new opportunities, possibilities, and realities. Although we retain the personality identity that we lived as in the physical life, we simultaneously discover and begin to experience our true multidimensional nature.

When this occurs, we may start to spontaneously know surprising truths about a vast array of topics and knowledge areas we previously had no interest in. These insights and intuitions come to us revealing surprising knowledge and wisdom that we didn't know we were aware of. We may see flashes of ourselves as other beings in different times and places and feel emotions and know the thoughts of these selves. However, these alter selves don't feel foreign or unusual, as we recognize ourselves in a multitude of forms.

We also experience others in a more multifaceted way. Through telepathy, which is the ability to transmit thoughts from individual to individual, we receive and send messages to those in both the spirit realm and the physical world. Able to detect when others are thinking of us, we are able to intuitively communicate with more than one being at the same time. Wherever we want to be, we can be, simply through intent or desire.

In this more expanded experience of self, we might find ourselves drawn to explore and learn from evolved masters and other advanced and enlightened beings. Areas of interest may include such things as exploring the cosmic Earth history and other planetary civilizations. We may desire to learn the higher truths within subjects such as math and the sciences, ancient spiritual teachings, and energetic, cosmic expressions of art and music. Many seek further advancement in intuitive, psychic development, higher-level magic, and a deeper understanding of energy manifestation and the energy body. We are drawn and invited into school-like environments based on our level of consciousness.

As we advance in unison with other souls, we become less self-based and merge with greater wisdom and love.

Soul Service Groups

After the soul review and restorative rest, we also have the opportunity to rejoin our soul service group. An aspect of our greater soul family, this body of souls works together to assist, support, and empower one another in service to the greater good. Some of our family members and friends may be part of our service group, along with other souls who we didn't know in our physical life. However, there is an instantaneous sense of knowing that we experience when in their company. Communication within the service group is a sharing of thoughts and inspiration through intuitive connection.

Every soul is an individualized facet of the divine and seeks to fully experience and express its unique contribution within the service group. Like the petals of a flower, all of which are connected around the same center, a soul service group draws its purpose and direction from the divine source. Service groups stimulate our higher knowing and wisdom and lift our hearts into greater harmony with one another and the divine. We are energized and feel freer and more whole when we are in the company of the other souls within our service group.

The timing of when we join our soul spirit group varies greatly and is determined by our level of consciousness. We can slow down our evolutionary process or speed it up. Much of this depends on the progress we've made in healing and integrating the experiences and challenges from our physical life. As we evolve in love and forgiveness, our vibration becomes stronger and we ascend to higher levels of awareness and freedom. When we are ready, we naturally gravitate toward our soul service group.

There are innumerable soul service groups, and each has a particular focus and area of service. Its members have expertise and gifts that enhance and complement other members' and strengthen the group's overall direction and purpose. Each of the souls within a service group share patterns of evolution and destiny and have come together through this attraction. Like a school of fish or a flock of geese making their way in the skies, the service group works as one unit, receiving telepathic communication and directions from a higher source.

As a multidimensional force, the service group transcends the physical limitations of time and space. While we are in the physical body, we fail to recognize that some of our interests, drives, and sense of purpose come to us by way of our service group. Our desire to help others and promote humanitarian, scientific, or creative causes and projects may be motivated by our soul service group.

Even though we are spiritually always at one with our service group, we may not be sharing the same experiences. Some souls in our group may be in the spirit realm and others in the physical world. Wherever we are, we continue to work for our common goals through our individual contribution, even when we are not aware that we are doing so.

Our experiences during our individual sojourns into the physical world play a role in the overall mission and purpose of the group. Our growth, joy, and triumphs benefit the whole. In return, our soul service group assists, supports, and guides us during our physical life through helping us to be in the right place at the right time to take advantage of opportunities, meet supportive others, and acquire essential information. Ideas, insights, motivation, and guidance from our service group come to us through our dreams, intuition, spontaneous knowing, and synchronicities.

For the most part, we earthly beings are unaware of the presence of our soul service group helpers in the spirit realm. Even though we are here on earth, we are part of a larger mission and purpose. In the physical world our contributions appear to be singular, yet we all have invisible helpers guiding our every step. We assume that the sudden awareness of ideas, inventive solutions, inspired actions, and general good luck are solely our own. However, you might say that it takes a cosmic village to create success, joy, and abundance.

Through the lens of the finite physical world, inter-dimensional communication and activity might not make much sense and seem impossible. However, our awareness here is limited. We aren't able to always be aware of the powerful force of love that is constantly working toward the good here and in the spirit realm.

New Talents and Interests

The gifts and talents of a soul service group are diverse, multifaceted, and birthed from infinite possibilities. Some soul service groups focus their efforts on understanding and advancing universal knowledge and applying this to specific areas in the physical world such as medicine, science, engineering, New Age and other spiritualities, technology, volunteer organizations, philosophy, music, art, the environment, and politics. Some groups are devoted to helping souls make the transition from the physical to the spirit realm, as well as caring for and healing those who pass over due to drug or alcohol addictions, suicide, trauma, or mass catastrophic events. Soul service groups might also explore other galaxies or star systems and may focus their efforts on other planets and with non-Earth beings of higher evolution. The physical realm is also aided by other planetary service groups who offer alternative forms of intelligence and innovative insights.

Every soul service group emits its own vibration which, combined with all other groups, harmonizes and reverberates throughout the cosmos. Within the wondrous harmony of our soul service group, we flow into greater unity with the divine all that is.

When we pass over we have the opportunity to rejoin our service group, review our contributions from the physical life, and continue in the group's higher purpose. We may advance into a new role or be given the opportunity to refine and develop other talents and gifts within the group. Some may choose to temporarily join a different service group to learn and explore. Although we all eventually take on our group's activities, we have free will and may choose to focus on supporting and comforting our family and other loved ones, both in the physical and spirit realms, before jumping into higher-level projects. Alternatively, some souls quickly rejoin their soul service group and get right to work.

For instance, David came in for a session and was so excited by his reading, he gifted his partner, Bob, a session for his birthday. During the session I was struck by Bob's desire to harness the power of the wind and the sun as alternative sources of energy. His devotion and interest in inventing and building both small and large effective renewable energy technologies was impressive. Although he had big and genius-like ideas, he was having a hard time raising the needed money to get his ideas, inventions, and products to the market. We talked at length about how to finance his work and received helpful guidance from his guides in the spirit realm.

Several years later, David contacted me for another session. He sadly told me that Bob had passed over quite unexpectedly one evening in his sleep. Although he had never had any issues with his heart, the cause of death was a massive heart attack.

In our session, Bob came in quickly and had a lot to share with David. He seemed grateful to be able to better communicate with him, and as he spoke of past fond memories and teased him about his love of exotic food and Chinese culture, I saw David shed a few tears.

After a short pause, his energy changed a bit and became a little more intense.

"Bob is showing me an image of a grid of energy surrounding the planet. He says that there are certain spots of this grid that build up pressure and can also be used as portals. His soul group helps to release the buildup of negativity and channel positive life-force energy back into the earth's atmosphere through these portals. He's learning how to diffuse rising tensions and replenish the natural world. Bob says that he is also sending positive energy and informative suggestions to people in the physical world who can fund and influence the creation of alternative energy sources. He says that there are many service groups with many souls who are helping to inspire those on the planet to make loving, kind, and wise choices for their well-being and the health of the planet," I said.

As Bob shared this information, I felt his dedication and saw glimpses of the shining pinholes of the light grid surrounding the earth that he described.

"It's good to know that he's doing what he always wanted to do. He was almost obsessed with his desire to create change. Yet, there always seemed to be one thing or another that blocked his path. I know that he loves being able to make a positive difference," David said.

Over the years of communicating with the other side, many souls have shared that they, too, are busy and involved in projects and activities that benefit people and the earth's environment. In addition to helping the planet detoxify and survive, others have shared their involvement in politics, science, the arts, and crisis issues, such as health epidemics, war, and mass starvation. There are others who have spoken of advancing medical research and promoting the connection between mind, body, and spirit healing and wholeness.

During our earth life many of us gravitate toward, have an interest in, or work in the area or field that our soul service group is focused on. However, not all of us here on earth are actively pursuing our soul service group's particular emphasis in our present lifetime. Instead, we may be more engaged in our personal growth and healing or other soul experiences. However, on the other side, we will at some point in our development naturally merge our efforts and energy with other souls for the highest good of all, both in the spirit world and the physical.

Fulfilling Our Purpose on the Other Side

As we become aware of the greater possibilities and are drawn into higher states of awareness and greater service on the other side, we are pulled toward what speaks to our heart. Some souls are surprised to discover that what they had wanted to experience and participate in while in the physical world is now more possible on the other side. It is never too late to engage our soul in its greater calling.

Although the physical life offers unlimited possibilities and creative opportunities, it also has limitations. Here in the finite world, we must work within the restrictions of time and space and other constraints. All too often, we are eager to advance and contribute to the greater good, but we find our path seemingly blocked. Despite our best efforts, we're not able to actualize and be of service in the way that we desire. Some experience frustration and a sense of failure when their efforts to participate in or achieve a goal don't happen in the way they thought they would. However, it is never too late; the spirit realm offers possibilities without end.

Although we might feel a particular calling and purpose in our earth life, our soul plan might include other priorities. We may have come here to work through more subtle issues and heal self-defeating beliefs and emotional patterns. At times we are here on earth to support others in fulfilling their dreams and goals and learn selflessness through this devotion. However, the wonder of the heavens provides an avenue to create our soul's desires.

For instance, Patti first came to see me for help with life direction. A wife and mother, she worked in the human resources department at a technology company but felt unfulfilled. After college she chose not to pursue graduate school in order to support her husband through law school. Now two children and many years later, she felt stuck. Although she did not regret raising her children and supporting her husband in his career, she wanted to pursue her own aspirations. She just wasn't sure what they were.

A short time after we started working together, Patti was diagnosed with breast cancer. Fortunately, the small tumor had not spread, and her prognosis was good. The cancer was slow growing, and her doctors were confident that she would have a full recovery.

While undergoing treatment, which included surgery, then chemotherapy, she had a spiritual awakening. In what felt like a flash of intuitive clarity she realized that her illness was a wake-up call to realize her deeper dream and desire to contribute to the world in a more meaningful and personal way. As soon as she was strong enough, she started to volunteer at a children's hospital and fundraise for cancer research. A year later, she left her job and decided to go back to school to get a dual degree in social work and divinity.

Patti was convinced that this was her spiritual calling, and she looked forward to being able to help others and make a difference in her community. However, a few weeks before school was to begin, another tumor was discovered during a routine checkup. After a biopsy and further exploration, her doctors found that her cancer had returned and spread. She immediately started treatment and postponed starting school.

However, she never got the chance. Less than a year later, she passed over at home surrounded by her family. A year or so later, her son came in for a reading. Patti was eager to share her love with him and commented on such things as his recent activities in school and dating. When her son asked her what it was like on the other side, she explained how she was helping young people who were experiencing challenges and suffering here in the physical world.

"Your mother says that before she passed over, she so much wanted to be of service to others, and she didn't think she would ever get this opportunity. However, she wants you to know that she is immersed in God's love and able to fulfill this desire and purpose. She says that she helps and guides people in the physical world who are feeling lost or suffering. She shows me an image of herself close to those in the physical world who are feeling lost, are in pain, or are suffering. It looks like she surrounds them in love and protection and whispers encouraging and comforting thoughts to them. She also transmits positive energy into their energy field and heart. Your mom says that she is part of a larger network of souls devoted to helping heal those in the physical world. She wants you to know that she is happy and at peace and wants you to remember that she is always by your side. No matter where you go or what you do, she is with you. She also says that it is okay to go away to graduate school; your dad will be okay."

Tommy was silent for a moment.

"That's what my mom wanted most, to help others. I'm glad she found this and that she's happy. She deserves it…I've wanted to go cross-country to grad school but didn't want to leave my father. I'm glad my mom is giving me a thumbs-up."

Sojourns to Other Planets

On the other side there are unlimited opportunities and no end to what is possible. As creation continues to unfurl its banner, joy rebounds through all existence. Life on the other side is never stagnant; we're always being pulled by the divine call of evolution. As we expand our sense of self and realize our multidimensional nature, we may sojourn to other planets and star systems where we absorb the specific energy that they radiate.

For instance, astrologically, we call Venus the planet of love for good reason. It holds and expresses the vibration of compassion and unconditional love. When a soul experiences unsatisfying relationship patterns in the physical world and has been challenged in receiving and giving pure love, they might visit the planet Venus to soak in its love vibrations and heal. Along with absorbing the energy of compassion and love, there are master teachers present who assist us in uncovering karmic wounds and unsatisfying emotional patterns that have carried through many lifetimes. Harmony is restored, and we learn how to better generate and maintain love and compassion within our spirit. We can then better express and receive this love from others. As we embody this love and healing, we often transfer and send it to our family and friends still on Earth.

In addition to Venus, we may journey to the moon to advance our intuition and bring our emotional energy into balance. Mercury offers us the opportunity to clear and expand our mental energy and communication. Mars helps us to balance our drive and brings equilibrium to our emotions. Many who were overly assertive or engaged in war work out these issues on Mars. Pluto assists us in becoming comfortable with our power while supporting our ability to transform and move into new ways of being. Jupiter is an expansive planet where we can experience rapid growth and come into alignment with our deepest wisdom. Saturn can empower us to become more disciplined and encourages us to confront our challenges and fears. Some who tried to escape from, or were in denial about, their earthly lessons find themselves on Saturn. We may travel and stay for a time in the vibrations of Uranus to express and become more aware of our individuality and become able to change and go with the flow. When we need additional healing in a calm and beautiful environment, we often journey to Neptune to soak in its calming and sublime vibrations.

In the physical world we tend to only view life and consciousness as a physical phenomenon. We are mistaken in our belief that Earth is the only planet inhabited by other life forms and souls. Although other planets may not be able to support the kind of physical life that we have on Earth, every planet is teeming with activity and gifts and holds an energetic vibration from which we can learn and expand our awareness.

Our loved ones on the other side are safe, active, and experiencing joy. Allow this truth to sink deep into your bones and your soul. Let it lift you to a greater understanding and acceptance of the joy that all of life offers. There is no death, only change and brief passages where we seem to walk alone.

Your loved ones are with you, offering their love and renewed awareness. In the next section you'll learn how to know when they are present and better communicate and connect with them.

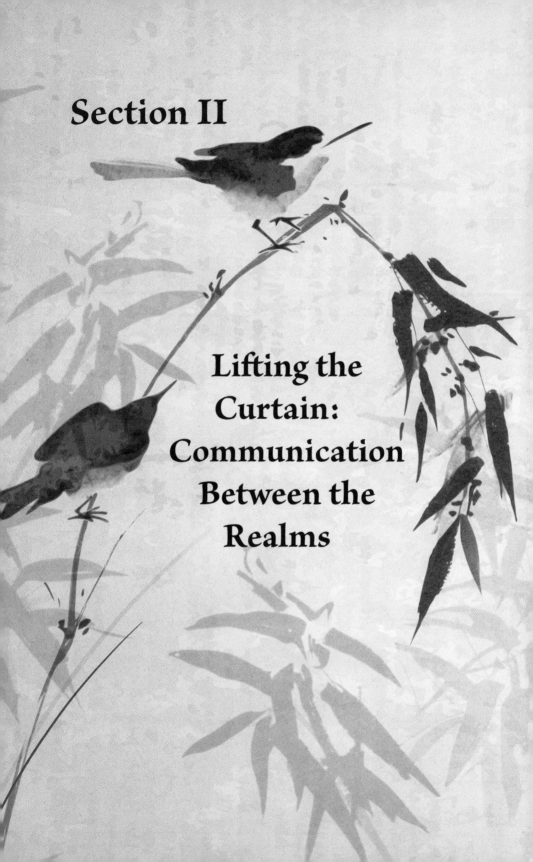

Section II

Lifting the Curtain: Communication Between the Realms

Chapter 6

Grief as a Passage
to Spiritual Intuitive Awareness

There is quite a contrast between what we experience in the physical realm after a loss and what our loved ones on the other side encounter soon after passing over. On the other side, our loved ones are held in the healing, divine light of an all-encompassing love. They come close to those they left behind in the physical world and whisper messages of comfort in our ear. Unfortunately, we usually aren't aware of their presence. Instead, after the loss of a loved one we may be feeling the depths of sorrow and loneliness, wondering if we will ever see or be close to our loved one again.

We have very little to go on when a loved one physically dies. Our human understanding of physical death doesn't offer us any explanation as to where our loved ones have gone and what is happening to them. We don't know if they cease to exist, if they have gone to a kingdom of heaven, or if they are still by our side. Our five senses cannot help us out, and there is no technology that allows us to interact and be aware of the other side. Maybe more than ever, we realize our limitations. Our loved ones are gone and we are here, left with the unknown and no answers.

In Between Here and the Other Side

The death of a loved one changes us. Through the loss of those we love, we come face-to-face with the truth that our world is temporary and transitory. Sorrow slowly winds through our heart, mind, and soul, and we experience our aloneness and singularity. Yet, in this hollow depth, something within us may quietly and faintly get our attention. There may be no outer movement or discernible presence that we can see or feel. Yet, this quiet presence nudges us with questions that we may have never considered: Where is my loved one? Is he or she close? Can they hear or see me?

Although we may have no concrete answers to these types of concerns, we continue to wonder. In this place of unknowing, silent responses may slowly begin to surface. A subtle and gentle sense of knowing drifts into our hurting heart.

"I am here," it whispers. "I am with you."

Even with no evidence of reliability or confirmation of the source, these simple messages ring of truth and bring hope. The possibility that our loved ones are still alive, their smile still spreading warmth, and their journey continuing in a place so much better than what was left behind, opens us to possibilities.

Still the grief comes again, overflowing the shores of our fragile hope and sending us adrift into endless waves of emotion. However, little by little the quiet, warm presence returns, silencing the sorrow. In this faint ray of warmth from the other side, we may feel suspended in time and space, where there is no future that we can conceive of without our loved one and the past is no longer.

This is the sacred space of grieving where we live between the heavens and the earth. Our old life is over, yet we have no firm sense of who we are or where we are going. After a loss, it is natural and healthy to dwell in this unknown in-between space. As uncomfortable as it may seem, it allows us the time and space that we need to grieve. Some may need to spend hours in the quiet, feeling and allowing the past memories and thoughts of their loved ones to slowly move through their heart, mind, and soul. Others might have more of a need to be with other family and friends or focus on work and keeping busy. The shock of loss may trigger the need to take control of our life and environment, or we may become more passive and float along. After a loved one passes over, we may be surprised by our needs during the mourning process and its influence in every area of our life.

Grief Deepens Our Intuitive Sensitivity

As this in-between place amidst heaven and earth spreads open, possibilities that we may not have ever considered get our attention. The deep alchemy of grief and tears often opens an intuitive passage. As our heart fills with sadness and sorrow, our defenses are shed. In this raw and vulnerable state, we are often more intuitively aware and receptive. The feeling and sense that we are not alone, and that our loved one is close, may continue to spontaneously surface through subtle and continual occurrences. Sometimes it may be a comforting warmth or what feels like a gentle touch on our shoulder or hand that gets our attention. It is also possible to suddenly smell the scent of flowers or a loved one's perfume or aftershave lotion.

Initially these kinds of sensations, feelings, and awareness lift our spirits, and we are excited and sure that a loved one is reaching out to us. Unfortunately, all too often, we then begin to question and wonder if the unexpected awareness of our loved one is just a hopeful wish and nonsense. We may fear that we are being foolish, and we might not be ready to accept that there is life after death. After an initial encounter with a loved one on the other side, many become uncomfortable and intuitively shut down, bury their feelings, and sink back into sadness.

Even when we are not ready to completely believe that we experienced a spiritual connection with the other side, a part of us yearns for another encounter. The intuitive awareness of a loved one's presence, no matter how faint it may be or how much we may discount it, often marks a shift in the grieving process. When our intuitive knowing begins to surface and strengthen, and we allow for the possibility that there is life beyond the physical world, we begin to transform. Just the desire to connect and feel the presence of a loved one on the other side is enough to create the momentum for the union of souls in heaven and on earth. The spiritual meaning of death is transformation, both for those who pass over and for those left behind. Just as our loved one's awareness is evolving, our awareness of life beyond the physical world is also expanding to accommodate their presence.

Going back and forth between wanting to believe and communicate with loved ones on the other side and denying that this is possible is to be expected. Grieving is rarely a straightforward path. We go through ups and downs, and sometimes we get stuck. Everyone grieves differently and we need to go at our own pace. The key is to feel our feelings, whatever they may be. Although the immensity of grief can be overwhelming, just feeling the depth of our emotions for a moment allows the process to unfold.

Within grieving there is a wisdom and timeless mystery that we can never fully comprehend. Immersed in the depths of suffering that a loss brings our way, we don't always recognize that death presents us with an invitation for increased awareness of ourselves and life. If we listen deeply to our grief, our heart opens and new truth seeps in.

Embracing Our Intuition Here and on the Other Side

The veil that separates the physical and spiritual realms is a bit flimsier than we imagine it to be. Still, we may be a little apprehensive and unsure as to how to reach out and contact a loved one on the other side. Some begin by taking baby steps, such as asking for a sign from our loved one on the other side while still holding back our full belief and participation. Others hope to feel or even see their loved one's presence, either in a dream or while awake. At the same time, they are a bit fearful of what it would be like if a loved one actually appeared to them.

For others, the awareness that a loved one is present comes more easily. I've had clients casually tell me that they know when their father, mother, or other loved one is with them. They may sense them while engaged in everyday kinds of things such as driving or folding laundry. They might also feel them sitting next to them while they are on the patio listening to the birds or on the couch watching television. The intuitive awareness of a loved one's presence may be woven into the fabric of their day-to-day lives. Some who are comfortable and more aware of their loved one's presence go about their business, catching glimpses and sensing them from time to time. Meanwhile, many others hope that their loved ones are close by but can't be sure.

While some are unsure of their intuitive ability, there are others who are more confident in their intuition and comfortable reaching out to the other side. If you have been born with this kind of awareness, or have come to it over the years, feel yourself to be blessed. It's a gift to be able to transcend earthly beliefs and limitations and have a natural connection to the unseen. However, not everyone will be able to accept your ideas. Although you might feel at odds with your family or others' beliefs, there will come a time when your interests are embraced.

This is what happened when Joana, a physician's assistant, came in for a session. As she sat down and got her phone's recorder ready, I felt the presence of her father.

"I believe your father is here," I told her.

"Really? I wasn't sure that he would show up. He loved to make fun of my far-out ideas," Joana said.

"Your father says that he loves you just the way you are. He knows better now and recognizes the gift you brought into his life. He says that among the many positive things that you brought into his life, you tried to help him wake up and motivate him to be less judgmental. He knows that he was stuck in his ways and missed out on a lot of opportunities. He says that you always kept things interesting. He's showing me an image of you when you were younger. It looks like you're dressed in a robe of some kind, like an orange sari. Did you join an ashram when you were young?"

Joana laughed and said, "That's so funny he brought that up. I started to go to a Buddhist temple when I was in high school. My father thought I was losing my marbles and tried to get me to go see the priest at his church. He had everyone praying and trying to save me."

"Your father's laughing too and says that you always knew how to get his attention. He understands now that he needed a little shaking up. He says that he's sorry for teasing you and not taking your interests seriously. He could've learned a lot from you, he says."

"Tell him it's okay, but I appreciate it. I never thought I'd get an apology from him. Please thank him for me," Joana said.

"He hears you and knows how you feel. Your father says that you always had a sixth sense about people and many other things. He's always known this about you, and your ability to know things that you would've had no way of knowing scared him some. He knows he pushed you away and hurt you. He wants you to know that you were way ahead of him."

The reading progressed, and after Joana's father shared more of his insights, other loved ones came forward with messages.

Before the session was over, I asked Joana if she had any questions.

"I don't quite know how to ask this," she said. "I guess I just wonder why I was so different than the rest of my family. Most of my life, I've felt like I didn't belong—in school and now at my job. It's not been easy. Will it always be like this?"

"My guides are telling me that this was your choice. Before you were born into this life, you volunteered, more or less, to be a kind of maverick or change maker."

"A what? What is a change maker?" Joana asked.

"It's a soul who comes into life to expose others to new ideas and help them to grow. Families tend to follow similar emotional and mental patterns from generation to generation, so much so that it becomes a source of pride to think and do things in a similar way as past generations. While this might make some sense through the human perspective, the soul is always on a mission of creative expansion and expression. When a family, community, or even nation gets too stuck in their ways, it negatively impacts everyone. Lack of curiosity and creative exploration and a closed mind cause unhealthy inertia. Nothing grows in a sterile and limited environment. With the help of someone, an original and authentic being, there is the possibility of change."

Once in the spirit realm, our loved ones recognize that there were people who came into their life, maybe someone in their family or a friend, who introduced them to new ideas and concepts and opened doors to better understanding that we live on after death. However, these new ideas may have challenged their long-held beliefs and assumptions, and they might have judged those who expressed them as weird or strange.

Even though our loved ones may have never entertained the thought of communication with the other side while in the physical world, they now see things differently. It doesn't matter if your loved one was comfortable using their intuition during their physical life or if they were more skeptical and wary of the idea. Like Joana's father, who was not a believer in his physical life, our innate intuition wakes up on the other side.

If you have an interest in life after death or communicating with the other side, some loved ones may not share and fully support this perspective. However, you are not as alone as it may seem. Although you may not always be aware of your loved ones on the other side, they are doing all they can to guide and comfort you. They are also learning how to improve their ability to better connect with you and get your attention. Just as we may need to learn and practice how to become better aware of those on the other side, they, too, are perfecting their ability to communicate with us here in the physical world.

Once our loved ones are on the other side, they more fully recognize the value of a spiritual consciousness while here on earth. They perceive the deeper meaning and purpose underlying what they experienced and understand how a spiritual perspective could have provided them with comfort, insight, and guidance. They might also become aware of the opportunities they had but missed to further explore and develop their awareness of the vast and beautiful web of life that lies beyond the physical. Our loved ones want to share the joy that they are experiencing on the other side and let us know that they are still with us.

The next chapter will help you to move through any blocks that might be getting in the way of your intuitive awareness and better recognize and discern your loved one's messages.

Chapter 7

Moving Through
Spirit Communication Obstacles

Love never dies and goes away. It simply changes and evolves. As our loved ones move through the soul review and further integrate with their higher soul energy, the love they share with us changes and transforms. Because of this, we may not always recognize it when our loved ones are close. We expect the feel of their presence to be similar to how we remember them to be, but this is not always the case. Although they still retain their personality, our loved ones on the other side have evolved and are now fueled by the pureness of their spirit and not the ego. Because of this, their presence often feels gentler, more comforting, and more calming than we might have remembered it to be.

Our loved ones on the other side are aware of what we are experiencing. They are near and watching over us, feeling our feelings and aware of our thoughts and our soul plan. They understand how our relationship with them continues and that from the spirit realm they can be a source of love, inspiration, healing, and strength. In the physical world, we are not as aware of our loved ones after they pass over.

Reaching out to a loved one in the spirit realm is an act of trust and faith. We aren't able to always see and hear them with the same clarity that they now possess. Despite a lack of assurances and proof of life after death, or the sure guarantee of a loved one's presence, it is only the intensity of our grief that may impel us to try and communicate with them. Loving is always a choice, and just as we learn how to best express love to others in the physical world, we must learn and practice what it means to love another who is on the other side.

This adventure into inter-dimensional love heals, comforts, and helps us evolve and become aware of our eternal, soulful self. When a loved one passes over, we are called to step into another expression and dimension of love's sublime beauty. Unfortunately, we often have unconscious or unknown obstacles that prevent us from connecting with our loved ones after they pass over.

To fully feel the presence of our loved ones and benefit from their love, we may need to remove the barriers that get in the way of fully opening and allowing love to enter.

Common blocks and obstacles that may prevent us from reaching out to the other side include such things as fear of the spirit realm, an increase in grief and sorrow as we open our heart to the other side, and regret, guilt, and confusion.

Letting Go of Fear

Some who believe that their loved ones live on after death might want to reach out and connect with them, yet they find themselves riddled with fear. For those who don't believe in the afterlife or that it is possible to communicate with the other side, the barrier of fear is even more of an obstacle. We humans tend to have a deep-seated fear of the unknown and what might happen if we open the door to the other side. We imagine that the spirit realm might be filled with tempting, tricky, and dark spirits and other paranormal creatures. However, these mean-spirited and evil-doing beings are for the most part created from the stuff of our imagination and usually resemble those characters that we read about or see in scary books and horror movies.

Our fears of the other side stem from our ego, which would love for us to run as fast as we can from anything that it cannot control. Please know that the other side has more beauty, love, compassion, and kindness than we can ever imagine. It may be called heaven, the light, paradise, the Summerland, or nirvana, and it is our soul's home. Our loved ones come to visit us from this place of love to express and share what they have discovered. They love us with a freeing love that heals, enlightens, and forgives.

If you choose to be brave and reach out to your loved ones on the other side, your life will change for the better. To connect with them, you don't have to be an expert medium and hear fully understandable messages or see your loved ones sitting next to you. A little openness, curiosity, and willingness to step into the unknown goes a long way. Your courageous effort to open the door and allow for the possibility is enough to make wonderful things start to happen.

EXERCISE
Opening Your Heart, Releasing Fear

If you feel that fear might be getting in the way of your reaching out to a loved one, here are some suggestions:

- Recognize that fear might be getting in the way of feeling the presence of your loved one. If you feel resistance to opening your heart, take some quiet time to feel and get in touch with your emotions. Feeling and naming our emotions helps free us from confusion and gives us the clarity to move forward.

- Write down your fears. Be honest and take some time to recall what you may associate with death. This might be childhood beliefs, scary movies, religious messages, or a discomfort with the unknown. You may discover fears that you didn't know existed and repressed subconscious beliefs. Just becoming aware of these unknown fears can free you from them.

- It can help to talk to someone about your fears, or seek input from others who have lost a loved one, and learn how they coped with their apprehension about connecting with them. Take a look at your fears and explore their origins and the hold that they have had on you. Know that you now have a choice to keep allowing your fears to hold you back or to release them.

- Find a quiet place and breathe and relax. Hold a loved one's photo or personal object in your hand. Remind yourself how much you love him or her, and spend some time allowing this love to surface. Find comfort in knowing that your loved one lives in this perfect love and that where there is love, there is no fear.

Moving Through Grief

Along with our fears, the overwhelming immensity of grief we experience after a loss can also prevent us from opening to the love of the other side. This is likely the most common reason that we are not able to feel the presence of our loved one after they have passed over. Grief can act as vibrational static and prevent clear intuitive receptivity. Although it's difficult to feel our feelings, as we allow the grief to surface, it flows through us and lessens. You will find that if you allow yourself to feel your feelings, your intuition will be stronger and clearer than it has ever been.

Although we often primarily feel sadness and grief after a loved one passes over, it is also normal and natural to experience other emotions as well. Similar to our loved ones on the other side, we are emotionally transforming and clearing. Sometimes emotions like anger, guilt, and even happiness surface. Don't feel shame for whatever you feel. Our mind, heart, and soul know how to grieve. Trust and let go into this inner wisdom; listen and follow what comes to the surface and allow it to guide you. You're not alone. There are powerful forces with you even when it feels the darkest. Ultimately this is a journey of transformation that leads to the awakening of aspects of your soulful self that may have been dormant and unknown.

As you move through the darkness of loss into the light of renewal, be aware of when you pull in and close your heart. Sometimes the grief is so intense we can't bear to continue to feel it. At times we may need to surface and come up out of the depths of sadness. It might help to do such things as spend time with friends and family, go to a movie, take a walk or go to the gym, read a book, play online computer games or crossword puzzles, or watch funny videos.

While it may be necessary to distract yourself from the intensity of grief, don't forget to continue to embrace and trust the grieving process. Be aware of when you emotionally shut down and become numb to the pain of loss for an extended period. While it may initially seem that shielding ourselves from the intensity of our grief is a good idea, it ultimately keeps us stuck and unable to heal.

If you feel overwhelmed with the sadness of loss, or if you suspect that you are emotionally shutting down and becoming depressed, try this meditation.

MEDITATION
The Core of Grief Is Love

Become comfortable, breathe long, deep breaths, and exhale any stress or tension. Continue to relax and ask for the presence of a family member, friend, or partner on the other side with whom you share a loving relationship. Feel the love that you share with him or her.

As you continue to breathe, imagine that your loved one is sending you love. Feel if there is any resistance to receiving it. Be aware of the tendency to pull inward and close your heart. If this happens, continue to breathe and imagine your heart opening. If you feel grief or pain, allow it to move through you. Don't resist; feel your feelings and release them through the exhale.

When we open ourselves and feel the love that we share with someone on the other side, we might begin to feel sad, or intense grief may surface. If this happens, allow yourself to feel whatever emotion needs acknowledgment and relief. It may take some time to feel lighter and for the intensity to subside. You might need a few minutes, or you can allow this process to occur over days or weeks.

When you feel the emotions lighten a bit, move your awareness into your heart and rest there. Become aware of the loving feelings that you have for your loved one on the other side. Breathe into these feelings and allow them to fully surface. Imagine your love as a fragrant rose coming into full blossom. Fully feel this love.

Send gratitude to your loved one for helping to nurture this love within you. Together you called this love into being, and it still exists and continues to strengthen. Feel this love and recognize that time and space cannot diminish or extinguish it.

As you soak in this love, become aware of any messages that your loved one sends to you. This may come through as a repetitive thought, word, or phrase, the soft feeling of their presence and comfort, the sensation of their touch, or shivers of energy up your spine or through your heart. You might also inwardly hear a message. A particular song might come to mind, or they might send you a message through images that are either symbolic or literal.

When we let go of the parameters of love and give it free rein outside of the limitations of the physical world, it lifts us into a higher vibration beyond time and space. This is the love that you now share with your loved one. When you accept your capacity to love and to allow love to flow through you, you form an eternal soulful bond with your loved one in the spirit realm. Love is not dependent on the things of this world and can never be limited or fully defined by it. When we love with the big love of the cosmos, blessings and miracles flow into our lives.

Guilt, Regret, and Confusion

It is quite common to feel regrets, confusion, and guilt when a loved one passes over. There is always something that we could have done differently or better, or conversations we could have had but didn't. Most of the people I work with hold on to something that they could have done, should have done, or didn't do. They may feel an immense amount of regret, guilt, and confusion and become preoccupied with these thoughts and feelings. Holding on to things that you could have done differently, regrets, and guilt can be a way to stall and repress the grief and loss that we feel. We may want to beat ourselves up and blame ourselves as a way to feel a sense of control over the confusion and guilt we feel.

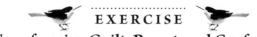

EXERCISE
Transforming Guilt, Regret, and Confusion

We are human and we make mistakes. Our attempts at love and intimacy often fall short of the ideal. Remind yourself that you did the best that you could at the time. If you find yourself overcome with guilt and regrets, here are some suggestions:

- Write down what is bothering you and what you may feel guilt, shame, or confusion about in your relationship with your loved one. Go into detail and pour out your feelings.

- Talk to someone you trust. Tell them what you did or didn't do that you regret or feel guilty about. Just hearing ourselves speak gets the thoughts out of our head and gives us a new perspective.

- Have compassion for yourself. We don't know why things happen the way that they do. Be kind to yourself. Imagine that a friend or someone you care about confessed to you similar guilt and regrets. What would you say to them? How would you feel toward them? Treat yourself with the same understanding and compassion.

- Close your eyes, breathe deeply, and relax. Open your heart and continue to breathe and relax. Imagine an image of your loved one who has passed over. Notice them in as much detail as you can, or simply get a feel for their presence. Communicate your feelings and express whatever issue or circumstance has caused you to feel guilt, confusion, or regret. You can say this aloud or send them a mental and emotional thought message. Ask your loved one for forgiveness. Tell them what you did or didn't do or say, and let them know what you would now do differently. Express whatever is in your heart that you would like them to know. Let them know that you didn't mean to cause them pain, confusion, or stress, and ask them to forgive you. Take a few moments of quiet. Breathe and open your heart and allow your loved one to love and forgive you. Become receptive and receive any messages from your loved one.

• Forgive yourself—this is what your loved one asks of you, needs, and wants you to do.

At times, grief, fear, and regrets will surface and block you from feeling and believing that your loved ones are present and with you. Recognize when these obstacles are present and be compassionate and kind to yourself. Grieving is a winding path that takes us through a multitude of emotions and insights. Practice these exercises whenever you feel a need and remember, even if you are not aware of a loved one's presence, they are close.

———

In the next chapter you'll be able to practice intuitively tuning in to your loved ones on the other side.

Chapter 8

Beginning Communication with the Other Side

Whether or not you realize it, your loved ones on the other side are communicating with you. As discussed in the previous chapter, the immensity of our grief after losing a loved one often plays a role in our ability to recognize and receive messages from our loved ones on the other side. Grief tends to cycle through varying degrees of intensity, and there is no time limit to grieving. Often the second year after a loved one's passing is more difficult than the first. The shock has worn off and life has slipped into a new routine. We may fear that we will forget the sound of their voice or the warmth of their presence. It's not unusual to experience some level of grieving years after a loss.

It is often when we are suffering through the most sadness and feelings of loss that we desire to connect and receive a message from a loved one. It's important to remember that our emotions may interfere with our ability to receive clear messages from the other side, but this doesn't mean that our efforts are in vain.

Before you begin to practice an intuitive exercise, take a moment to access your level of sadness, and if it is deep and profound, maybe limit your intuitive expectations. You can still actively intuit, as your loved ones will be able to see, feel, and know that you are reaching out to them. But be patient, as you may not be able to recognize an immediate response. However, when you least expect it and are in a more receptive state, you will likely receive answers and recognize the connection and presence of your loved one.

Let Go of Assumptions

It's easy to make an assumption as to how and what a message from a loved one will be. Try to keep a curious and open attitude as to what you will experience when you communicate with the other side. Quite often we spontaneously send and receive messages without realizing it. As we become aware of when and how we are intuiting, it becomes easier to know when our loved ones on the other side are close, and how to better interact and communicate with them.

Those on the other side live outside of the limitations of the physical five senses. They can see and hear us much better than we can see and hear them. It delights them when we reach out, and they reciprocate and try to let us know they are present. Emotional energy is powerful and what is said with love, desire, and longing, reaches your loved one. In some way, you will get a response. However, it might not come at the time or in the form that you expect or hoped for.

For instance, you might be grocery shopping a day or so after attempting to converse with your loved one and out of nowhere a thought, sensation, or feeling that you know is from your loved one floats into your awareness. When we notice these gentle intuitive messages from the other side, our heart might fill with the love and awareness that we are not alone. However, sometimes we want to believe but doubt our intuitive ability and discount what we receive.

The desire for concrete proof and verifiable evidence that our loved ones are with us is common. When I communicate with those on the other side, I offer my clients personal details and descriptions such as a physical description of their loved one, a name, or the illness or cause of death. This provides them with assuring evidence that their loved one is present.

However, tuning in to our own loved ones on the other side is not as straightforward. We know and are familiar with them, and it's not always easy to sort out our own thoughts and feelings from the messages that our loved ones are sending us. Our loved ones are still very much a part of us, even after physical death. They are so close, in fact, we aren't always able to distinguish their thoughts and feelings from our own.

How You May Be Communicating with the Other Side and Don't Know It

Everyone is capable of receiving intuitive messages from those on the other side. You don't have to be a medium or highly intuitive to have the sense and feeling that a loved one is close. Through the synergy of love, you share a connection with loved ones that time, space, and physical death cannot erase.

Intuition is a natural sense that we all possess, and it is as unique as we are. Over the years of giving readings and teaching others to develop their intuitive ability, I've found that our intuition surfaces through four common modalities. When connecting to our loved ones on the other side, it is helpful to be aware of how our natural intuition surfaces. The four primary ways that we unknowingly connect with our loved ones are through our thoughts and a sense of knowing, through our emotions and feelings, through our physical body, and through our energy field. Although most people have one or two primary ways of intuiting, we are usually a combination of all of the types.

(In my books *Discover Your Psychic Type*, *You Are a Medium*, and *You Are Psychic*, you can learn more about the characteristics and personality tendencies for each type and how to develop and better use your intuition.)

Sharing Thoughts (Mental Intuition)

If you're not sure how to approach your loved ones on the other side, just begin to talk to them. You don't need to know for certain if they are with you. When you direct your intent to communicate with them, they will be close. You can send them a thought message by just thinking a thought and imagining sending it to them. You can communicate and talk to them aloud or silently within your mind. It might not feel very supernatural to simply open up and start a conversation with the other side, and you might have to get over your fear of feeling a bit kooky. However, it can be this simple. Share your concerns, ask for advice, and tell them you love them. Your loved one feels your feelings and hears your concerns, and they love it when you talk to them.

Have you ever suddenly known that a loved one is communicating with you through your thoughts? We often receive intuitive messages through inner hearing or by carrying on an inner dialog with a loved one without knowing it. Mental intuition can sometimes feel like we are talking to ourselves or making up a conversation in our head. A loved one's thoughts can be subtle and not seem different from our own.

If you primarily communicate with the other side through thought messages, getting into a relaxed state and emptying the mind of the thoughts and concerns of the day can be helpful. Just breathe, exhale, and when your mind starts to wander, keep focusing on the breath. This will clear your mind and allow messages to seep in.

Pay attention to the thoughts that drift in when you are engaged in a mundane task such as driving, mowing the lawn, or folding laundry. We are often intuitively receptive and naturally receive thought messages from our loved ones during these times.

Mental Intuitive Strengths While Grieving

While grieving, a mental intuitive might receive insights and guidance from their loved one on the other side through a sense of knowing and through their thoughts. These messages tend to be comforting, matter of fact, and often funny and friendly. While we often expect profound, deep messages, more often they are simple and help us to feel that our loved one is close. Most of the time, communication with the other side is easy and natural—so much so that we might not realize that we are conversing and connecting with the spirit realm.

Mental Intuitive Weaknesses While Grieving

Those who primarily intuit through mental intuition can at times have obsessive and repetitive thoughts after the loss of a loved one. This may include going over and over the details or circumstances of a loved one's passing and wanting more information or insights as to why and how they passed over. If you experience this, recognize that these kinds of thoughts are common, especially for those who primarily intuit through mental intuition. Underneath the mind chatter, there is grief and sadness. Allow your emotions to surface and feel them, even if it feels difficult. As you allow deep feelings of grief to be felt and released, repetitive thoughts will subside, and you will be able to better receive uplifting messages.

The Receptive Heart (Emotional Intuition)

As we've previously discussed, grieving, sadness, and loss affect our ability to receive clear messages from the other side. However, even in the depths of despair, love is still present. The love between ourselves and another is not limited by physical death. On the other side, love is like oxygen. It is everywhere and is the energy that supports us. Our loved ones are immersed in this great sea of divine love and send it our way.

An emotional intuitive tunes in to loved ones through the heart and emotions. Have you ever felt a loved one's presence as a comforting warmth, a surge of love, or as a heart-centered feeling of awareness? If you are inclined to feel your loved one's presence through emotional energy, you might for example feel comforted during a difficult time or feel a deep sense of peace in the midst of stress. Quite often our loved ones on the other side transmit loving feelings as a way to continue to care for and watch over us.

Emotional Intuitive Strengths While Grieving

When we pass over, we enter into the sublime, all-encompassing realm of love. Those who intuit primarily through their emotions tend to be more attuned to the higher vibrations of love. They are able to receive and feel their loved one's presence as love and comfort. Emotional intuitives can naturally help others who are grieving through their highly-evolved, heart-centered awareness and compassion.

Emotional Intuitive Weaknesses While Grieving

Those who intuit primarily through their emotions may be prone to projecting their worries and concerns onto their loved ones who have passed over. For instance, they might worry that their loved one felt fear, suffering, or stress while passing. They might worry that their loved one is alone, lost, or not feeling loved on the other side. An emotional intuitive might also be overwhelmed with the intensity of their grief after a loved one's passing and stuff down and repress their emotions. This can lead to depression, and if emotions are repressed for a longer period of time, this might cause health problems. If you are overwhelmed with feelings of grief, it might be helpful to pour out your feelings through journaling and share your feelings with a grief counselor or someone you can trust.

Taking In the Vibes (Physical Intuition)

As we pass out of the physical body, we realize that we are energy. Our energy body may look similar to our physical body, yet it is indestructible and fueled by the higher vibrations of divine energy. A physical intuitive receives energy information through gut feelings or physical sensations.

For example, a shiver of energy running up the spine, or the hairs on the arms standing up, may be an intuitive indicator that a loved one is near. Physical intuitives might also experience the sensation of comforting warmth on their shoulder or hand or smell the faint scent of a loved one's perfume.

Physical Intuitive Strengths While Grieving

Because a physical intuitive receives the energy of those on the other side through physical vibes, they may be able to tune in to a loved one through personal objects and photos. Holding a loved one's photo or piece of their jewelry, or being in their home, can open a channel for intuitive communication with the other side. The intuitive awareness that a loved one is present may also come more easily to a physical intuitive through noticing signs in the natural world that the other side has sent their way.

Physical Intuitive Weaknesses While Grieving

A physical intuitive is prone to unconsciously absorbing energy into their physical body. While grieving they may unknowingly suppress their own emotions and also take in the emotions of others who are grieving. This can lead to feeling lethargic and overly tired as well as experiencing bodily aches and pains and headaches. If you feel that you chronically lack energy, are tired, and feel numb while grieving, take a walk in nature, drink plenty of water, and eat well. It's important to keep your physical energy moving. It might also be helpful to talk to someone you trust or keep a journal of your feelings. It can be helpful to put words to your grief, as creative expression can be healing.

Spiritual Energy Awareness (Spiritual Intuition)

A spiritual intuitive receives and absorbs intuitive energy through the energy field. If you sometimes see images through inner sight or sense a presence close, you might intuit through your energy field. Even though most of us cannot visually see into the electromagnetic field, it is still very much a part of us and surrounds all living beings. While this may sound more abstract than the other types of intuition, remember that our energy body survives physical death and is the eternal part of us.

Spiritual Intuitive Strengths While Grieving

A spiritual intuitive is more comfortable with the idea of life after death and encountering spirits than the other types of intuitives. They naturally accept the reality of nonphysical life, and many easily sense or see the presence of loved ones close by. With this intuitive sensitivity you might also see shimmering or fleeting sparks of light or orbs when a loved one on the other side is present. It might be easy to dismiss these types of elusive phenomena. However, if you become receptive and inwardly listen when you see an orb or spark of light, you might receive a message from the other side. Spiritual intuition may also manifest through the awareness of a loved one visiting you in your dreams.

Spiritual Intuitive Weaknesses While Grieving

Because a spiritual intuitive is more attuned to the nonphysical realm, in times of loss and grief they might detach from their emotions and become spacey and not present. In extreme cases this can lead to a lack of self-care of one's physical needs, such as staying in bed for hours and days or forgetting to eat or eating too much. They might also become overcharged with energy and remain overly busy and distracted.

If you find yourself chronically losing track of time or having difficulty managing day-to-day issues over an extended amount of time, focus on the basics. Eat good food, pay attention to how much or how little you are sleeping, take a walk, drink plenty of water, and share your feelings with a counselor or someone you trust.

MEDITATION
Inviting a Loved One to Be Close

Your loved ones will send you love, messages, and comfort at random times. You may or may not always recognize and be aware when they are present and connecting with you. Being familiar with the four basic intuitive types will help you to better notice and tune in to the messages that come your way. Remember, we all have one or two types that are the most natural to us, but we can intuit through all four modalities interchangeably.

To further communicate with the other side, it can be helpful to become receptive, open, calm, and enter into a meditative state. Here is an easy exercise to practice:

- Get into a comfortable position in a quiet place and relax. Take a few long, deep breaths and exhale any stress and tension. As you continue to relax and breathe, imagine white light energy moving from the soles of your feet up through the body. At the same time, imagine that you are breathing white light energy down through the top of the head. Continue to breathe, relax, and fill yourself with this white light energy.

- As you inhale white light down through the top of the head and up through the soles of the feet, exhale it through the heart. Continue to breathe in white light and exhale it through the heart. As you do this, imagine this white light energy extends outside of your body and forms a translucent bubble that completely surrounds you.

- Continue to breathe and relax. When you feel the energy bubble around you strengthen, invite your loved one close, say their name, and ask for their presence. Be patient and continue to relax and open your heart. As you continue to breathe white light energy, pay attention to any images, feelings, thoughts, or sensations that you receive.

- Try not to overthink or have any expectations as to what you should or shouldn't be experiencing or feeling. Just surrender to the process, send love to your loved one, and remain receptive. Continue to receive without judgment or trying to figure out what you are receiving, and limit your expectations.

- Be aware of any thoughts that surface, especially if they are relative and even toned. Allow your heart to open and feel whatever feelings emerge. Pay attention to any bodily sensations such as tingling on your scalp or spine or waves of energy that seem to flow through you. Your loved ones might also send you flashes of light, orbs, or images. Don't discount whatever you see, feel, know, and sense. Breathe and receive it all.

- When you feel the energy begin to dissipate, thank your loved one for coming close and gently come into normal consciousness. You might want to write down whatever you receive, even if you are not sure if it is meaningful. In time you might gain new insights and awareness.

What to Expect

If you have watched a medium give a reading on a television show or have had a reading by a professional medium, you might expect to receive the same type of information that they do. However, communicating with your own loved ones is not the same as tuning in to someone else's. When we do not personally know who we are communicating with on the other side, the guidance and insight we receive is more objective and neutral. Because we are unaffected by grief and sadness, we are better able to fully trust our intuition and listen to it.

When we connect with a family member or with someone we were close to or knew as a friend or acquaintance, our experience will be more personal and subjective. With our own loved ones we are not going on a fact-finding mission, but a journey of love. Feelings of warmth, love, and forgiveness are likely, so much so that you may not be able to fully describe what you feel or readily put it into words. For some who would like clear guidance and messages, this might be a bit frustrating, and you might wonder if you are doing something wrong. Connecting with our own loved ones is more of an emotional and healing experience. It is almost impossible to be neutral, and our ability to always recognize the fine line between self-generated and intuitive information is more difficult. Our connection is more heart and soul.

When you tune in to their presence, a loved one might send you common intuitive messages such as:

- Feelings of warmth in the heart or in the body, shivers of energy running up your spine, or the hair on your hands or arms standing up
- The sense or knowing that a loved one is close
- Receiving insights into a current concern or issue
- Seeing a flash of light or sensing energy
- A spontaneous heart opening and sudden feelings of love and comfort
- Seeing an image of your loved one
- Suddenly hearing the lyrics of a song in your mind
- Smelling a loved one's perfume, aftershave, or the fragrance of flowers
- The inner feeling that everything is going to be all right or a feeling of inner peace

- Hearing a word, phrase, or sentence over and over
- Spontaneous laughter and perceiving things in a lighthearted and joyful way
- A bird coming to the window or hearing a bird call outdoors
- A bell, alarm, or your phone making noise

The spirit realm is clever and there are many other ways that a loved one will let you know that they are present.

If we allow ourselves to open and let go of expectations and overthinking, we are drawn into the web of synergy that bonds us to our loved ones. Our loved ones are outside of the limitations of the physical world, and their presence is transcendent. When we open our heart and mind, their messages more easily flow into our awareness. However, we may not always immediately feel the positive effects of this connection. Grieving can take time, and your loved one's influence may slowly distill within. Feelings of hope, a sense of renewal, a new direction, love, and comfort will eventually emerge.

———

In the next chapter you will discover a few other ways to tune in to your loved ones and how they may let you know they are present.

Chapter 9

The Varied and Creative Ways
Our Loved Ones Communicate with Us

The varied and creative ways that those on the other side employ to get our attention is limitless. We often desire direct intuitive communication with our loved ones; however, communication between the physical and spiritual realms is not always as straightforward as we would like it to be. It can be tricky to know with overwhelming certainty when a loved one is present. So be alert and open to some less common ways that they let us know they are with us.

Communication with the spirit realm is more art than science. It requires an open mind and heart and the adaptability to let go of expectations of how you think they will communicate.

Here are some common strategies that the other side tends to employ to get our attention:

Memories

When a loved one passes over, it is common to remember and review our past experiences with them. Our memories bring us comfort and can help us to feel closer to our loved ones. They can ease our grief and reignite within our heart the love and special magic that we shared with another. We can learn from our memories and understand another person or our relationship in new ways. As we process our grief and deep sense of loss, memories can help us cross the bridge from sorrow to peace.

Memories can also be a powerful form of communication with our loved ones on the other side. After a loss it might feel like all we have left are our memories. Crystallized within our memories is the joy, love, and laughter that we shared with another. Remembering good times with our loved ones can help us to feel close to them and have gratitude for all that they brought into our lives. Reminiscing about the past can also help us through the grieving process. When we recall and feel the positivity of our time with a loved one, we are often better able to understand and feel blessed by our journey together. However, we might also unconsciously resist remembering positive memories because we fear that recalling happy times might make our loss feel so much greater.

Another aspect of remembering the past to be aware of is the tendency to hold on too tightly to our memories. Reliving positive events from our time together might stall our ability to move forward in the grieving process. If you find yourself recalling past events over and over, remember that the joy you shared with your loved one is always in your heart, and their soul is alive and with you.

Along with good feelings, we also have memories that provoke feelings of guilt, regret, or sadness. At times, a particular memory might surface over and over, causing us distress. As we look back, we might wonder why we didn't do things differently, apologize, or better communicate our thoughts and feelings to our loved one. These kinds of memories can be common after a loved one passes. Extreme grief and the stress and anxiety of loss can stir up uncomfortable regrets and recriminations. If this happens it can be helpful to recognize that troubling and regretful thoughts may be a smokescreen, shielding us from feeling the profound depth of loss and sadness that we feel.

Memories As an Intuitive Tool

As our loved ones on the other side move through the soul review, they sift through past memories. While they are actively involved in this process, we might simultaneously remember memories similar to the ones that they are experiencing. This might seem improbable, yet it is more common than we know. Connected through our heart, soul, and energy field, we are one with our loved ones. When two people come together through love and devotion, the synergy creates a presence and being that is greater than either one. When a loved one passes over, our connection transforms and changes, but it doesn't dissolve.

Memories can be a form of intuitive communication that is more common than most realize. When a memory of a loved one makes its way into our consciousness, it is not always obvious that someone on the other side is transmitting this message to us. For instance, spontaneously recalling a memory of a time when a loved one comforted us or when we felt loved and safe might be an intuitive message. A loved one may be close and aware of a difficulty or challenge we are confronting, and they are letting us know that they are with us.

Sometimes a memory of an event from the past that involved a painful or confusing situation with a loved one might unexpectedly surface. Often our loved one is reviewing the past and might be requesting forgiveness for any hurt that they may have caused us. They might also be extending forgiveness for one of our past actions, or it may be a bit of both. Pay attention to the feelings and thoughts that occur while remembering the past. Memories can also provide insight for better understanding a past event or our loved one. If you recall challenges from the past, take a deep breath, open your heart, and allow yourself to feel the warm, soothing love that the spirit realm is sending your way.

One of the identifying qualities of a shared intuitive memory is the effect it has on us. Shared memories may include the recollection of positive and uplifting events that help us to feel our loved one's loving presence. Recalling times of joy and laughter can ease the sadness and grief of mourning and fill our heart with the most positive aspects of our relationship. Shared memories during the soul review might also include remembering pivotal events in our relationship. These memories provide us with the opportunity to look back at our journey with a loved one and better perceive how we supported, influenced, grew, and evolved together.

For instance, as soon as I started the session with Abby, I felt her mother's presence. As I described her and shared a few messages, I could feel Abby's heart open. It was clear that they had a close and loving connection. Before we ended the session, I asked Abby if she had any questions for her.

"I don't know if this question is for you or for her. Why don't I feel her close to me or get signs from her? I want to believe she is with me, but I can't feel her," she said.

Immediately, her mother replied. "Your mom says that she doesn't want to interfere. She shows me you, busy with work and your children, and she doesn't want to take your attention away from the many day-to-day things that you're doing."

"I would love to feel her presence," Abby said.

"Your mom is showing me you as a little girl, just a toddler. You had beautiful curly dark hair, and in this image it looks like you're outdoors. Maybe at a small pond or river. You're feeding ducks and your mom shows me you running after them…I'm not sure why she is showing me this. It doesn't seem to be answering your question."

"It is…I know why she is bringing this up. On my way to work last week, I had the same vivid memory. I was at a stoplight and this image popped up out of nowhere. We used to go to the lake near our home in the mornings to feed the ducks. It was a special time for me and my mom. We did it for years. Whenever we needed to talk or just be together…As I was remembering this, I felt a bolt of energy opening my heart, and I started to cry. I could feel how much my mother loved me, and it felt like she wanted me to know how much joy I brought her…I guess she is close."

EXERCISE

Receiving a Message from a Loved One Through a Memory

Memories from the other side often invoke deep emotions and open our heart with love and joy. However, even those memories that recall a challenging situation can lead to a new understanding of ourselves and our loved ones by giving insight into our present circumstances. If you suspect that a loved one has sent you a message through a memory, try this:

- Allow yourself to fully feel and embrace the memory. If you can, lie down or sit back, relax, and close your eyes. Recall the memory in as much detail as possible.

- Imagine yourself in it. What is happening? How do you feel? Fully feel any emotions and feelings that surface.

- At times, the memory might become more like a dream. It begins to change and unfold differently than what you remember in the original event. If this happens, trust the process and allow it to continue.

- As you recall and feel the memory, become receptive and allow any intuitive insights to surface. Your loved one may be using the memory as a way to convey a specific message.

- Even if the memory doesn't necessarily seem significant, take your time and savor it. Let it live in your heart and continue to unfold and speak to you. Pay attention to feelings of peace, comfort, and resolution. Quite often, messages from our loved ones are not intellectual but more emotional and comforting.

Dreams

Dreaming of loved ones after they pass over is common. Some of these dreams are created by our subconscious mind and support us in processing our emotions and working through the intensity of loss and grief. Over time, dreams of our loved ones can help us come to closure and move forward in rebuilding our lives.

Sometimes our loved ones who have passed over visit us in dreams. While we sleep, the conscious mind is no longer active, and we are often more able to receive messages from the other side. However, we don't always remember them. If you wake feeling comforted, more peaceful, and with the sense that a loved one may have visited you during the night, they likely did. Dreams of our loved ones can also be clear and vivid and feel more like a visitation. It might feel as if we can touch them, smell their perfume, and know their thoughts.

For instance, late one night, a hospice worker called Jeff to let him know that his mother's death was imminent. A short time later he was on his way to her home, a three-hour drive from where he lived. He had visited the weekend before and had thought about staying with her but decided to go home and take care of his cats and get a few things.

As he turned into his mother's pebbled driveway, he had an overwhelming feeling that he was too late. He knew in his heart that she had passed over. Sitting in his car watching the sun come up over the distant hills, guilt crept into his heart. He beat himself up for going back home and not staying with his mother after his last visit. She had passed over without him there and he couldn't forgive himself.

Later that night he dreamt about the day he left home to go to college. In this memory-dream, a couple of his friends who were attending the same college pulled into his driveway and honked the horn. Eager to get going, he almost forgot to say goodbye to his mother.

After running back into the house to give her a hug, he felt his mother close. He knew that she wanted him to be free and pursue his new life in college without worry or stress about her.

Waking from the dream, Jeff continued to feel his mother's spirit close. He felt that she was trying to tell him through this dream that it was time to let her go. Just as he rushed out the door ready to take on school and a new life, she left this earth ready for her next adventure.

Mimicking her encouraging words after he left for college, he said, "I love you, Mom, thank you. You go have fun, be free, and don't worry about me."

Dreams from Loved Ones During the Soul Review

While our loved ones are going through the soul review, we might also intuitively connect with them through our dreams. The content and emotional intensity of these dreams are different from a subconscious dream and usually involve the memory of a past event. However, the images and other characteristics may be more symbolic and not always resemble what actually happened. If a dream involves a loved one on the other side and stirs up emotional intensity from the past, it might be connected to a loved one's soul review.

For instance, my friend Larry had a dream that he was in his childhood home, only it didn't look much like the house he grew up in. Walking through the house, he came to a room that was empty except for a pair of worn slippers near a television set that was on but out of focus. Something about the slippers reminded him of his father and how he liked to watch TV while relaxing in his recliner in the evening. As an overwhelming wave of sadness came over him, the dream scene changed, and he found himself alone walking on an empty shoreline. In the distance he saw a man who he thought might be his father.

Waking up from the dream, feelings of sadness flooded Larry's heart. The intensity of his feelings reminded him of how during his childhood his father was usually too busy to show much interest in him or go to his games. Now that his father had passed over, he realized he would never get the time and attention from him that he had always longed for. Thinking about the dream, he wondered if the man in the distance was his father.

After tossing and turning a bit, he fell back to sleep and slipped into another dream. In it, his father stood on the ocean shore with an uncharacteristic and infectious smile. Larry could feel his father's regret for not making more time for him. It felt as if his father was sending him the message that he knew how lonely he felt as a child. As he continued to feel his father's remorse, he heard him ask for Larry's forgiveness. Warmth and love spread through Larry as he quickly and without reservation forgave his father.

EXERCISE
Invoking a Loved One's Presence in a Dream

If you would like to feel a loved one's presence and communicate with them through a dream, try this:

- Place a photo or other personal item of the loved one you would like to communicate with close to your bed. If you don't have a photo or personal item, write their name on a piece of paper.
- Before you go to sleep, fill your heart with loving feelings for them and imagine sending it their way.
- As you send love to the other side, send a thought message asking your loved one to visit and be with you in a dream. You can send them this thought message by speaking out loud or simply through thinking the thoughts. You can also imagine writing your request on a slip of paper and sending it to them.

Sometimes a loved one comes to us in a dream, but they don't look like they did before they went over. They might be older, younger, or may not appear anything like they did in the physical world. If you get the sense, feel, or know that a person or image in a dream is a loved one, don't overthink it, just assume that it is. Dreams from loved ones on the other side, especially dreams that are intuited during the soul review, tend to invoke deep emotion. This includes feelings of love as well as feelings of hurt or confusion from the past.

Although a dream may be inspired by a loved one, it may be more symbolic and not include realistic images from the past. However, even though a loved one may not look like they did in the physical world and you don't recognize the scene in the dream, that doesn't lessen its healing potential.

If you wake and feel that a dream may be noteworthy, even if you are not sure why, write it down. Sometimes just writing down a dream invokes and stimulates more intuitive information. Pay attention over the next few days and weeks, as more information and insight may spontaneously surface as well as a more tangible connection with a loved one in the dream. Even if you cannot decipher and adequately interpret a dream, it can still have a positive impact. Sometimes dreams stir up buried emotions that we need to release and let go of, or they can help us feel the kind of sublime closeness to our loved ones that we long for.

Photos and Videos

Another common but often overlooked way that loved ones communicate with us is through photos and videos. Similar to memories, photos can help us recall past events and stimulate feelings of love and comfort between ourselves and those on the other side. They might also contain a specific message and trigger intuitive receptivity. Photos and videos also hold an energetic imprint of whoever's image is captured.

For instance, before my mother passed over, she suffered for over a year with cancer. Once vibrant and full of energy, she became so emaciated before her passing that she couldn't stand or eat without help. For weeks after her passing I continued to imagine her in the thin, frail, and weak state of her illness. Even though I knew that once in the spirit realm she came back into her full, vibrant soul energy, I couldn't shake the images.

One afternoon my daughter found an old video taken years earlier that she wanted me to watch. In it my hair was made up in a popular style for that time and my daughter thought it was hilarious. After a little coaxing from her, I agreed to watch the video and see my ridiculous hairstyle. However, instead of my image, the video opened on my mother with a big pillow stuffed in the back of her pants dancing and singing a song with my daughter from The Jungle Book. She was having a great time, and in that surprising moment of seeing her, I knew that she was sending me a message. From then on when I thought of her, I saw her being her silly self and having a fun time on the other side.

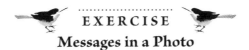

EXERCISE
Messages in a Photo

Some mediums require photos of loved ones on the other side in order to communicate with them. Photos absorb our energy vibration, and we can intuitively feel closer and connect with another just by looking at a picture of him or her. Objects that we wear or use over a long period of time also absorb our energy presence. The psychic ability to intuitively connect with someone through a piece of jewelry, their keys, or their photo is called psychometry.

Randomly go through photos of a loved one, allowing your intuition to guide you. When you come to one that you feel or sense has a message for you, pause, hold it, and close your eyes. If the photo is digital, place your hand over it, close your eyes, and relax and breathe.

Pay attention to any emotions, thought messages, tingles of energy, sensations, or gut awareness that you experience. Continue to relax and allow any feelings, memories, or new awareness to surface. As you do this, you might also feel the presence of your loved one and receive a message.

Music

Music opens the heart and helps us relax and become more fluid—the perfect state to receive intuitive information. Those on the other side often send us messages through music. This might come in the form of inwardly hearing a song or lyrics or turning on the radio while a familiar and meaningful song from the past is playing. At times we might encounter familiar songs from our loved ones playing in a supermarket while we shop, during a concert, or in another public place. The music that our loved ones send us usually conjures up memories of a special occasion or events we shared with them. Shivers of energy might run up our spine as our heart opens and we breathe in the essence of their heavenly love.

On the other side, there is a constant soft and gentle, harmonic and soothing vibration. As a musician, Kenni, my ex-husband on the other side, was particularly sensitive to sound—so much so that we had to give up going to theaters. If the audio system was not balanced to perfection, he would wince uncomfortably in his seat until we went in search of another place to sit.

Since his passing over, I inwardly hear the harmonious music of the heavens drift through me every now and then. Music on the other side is not just heard but felt. It's a full soul experience where waves of high-vibration energy move through us and we become the instrument. Moving with the breath of the divine is truly a holy experience.

EXERCISE
Music as a Messenger

If you feel that you may be receiving intuitive messages from the other side through music, try this:

- If you inwardly hear a familiar tune or song lyrics that remind you of a loved one on the other side, take a moment to relax and open your heart. If it's possible, sit or lie down and close your eyes.
- Allow any feelings or thoughts to surface. Breathe deep, relaxing breaths and become receptive.
- Imagine that your loved one has a message for you. You might also feel a loved one's presence as a warm feeling of love or comfort.
- You can also open the lines of communication to a loved one on the other side by listening to a song or music that had special meaning for the two of you.
- Become comfortable, close your eyes, and as you listen, send a message to your loved one. Continue to relax and pay attention to any response you receive from the other side.

Sometimes the response will not come immediately, but hours or days later when you are not expecting it, a loved one might send you a song in response.

Emotions

When we lose someone with whom we shared a loving, trusting, and joyful connection, their love may seem gone forever. Without their warm touch, smile, and physical presence, we may feel lost and wonder if we will ever again feel the kind of closeness, love, and connection that we shared with him or her.

Grieving the loss of a loved one can take us into a depth of emotion that we didn't know existed. Emotions are powerful, especially those that emanate from the pure recesses of our heart. After a loss, we can feel alone and adrift, tossed about by waves of sadness, confusion, and loneliness. When experiencing the intense emotions of grief, it can feel as if we have been plunged deep into the darkness with only brief respites from the pain.

Whatever you feel when a loved one passes over is natural. Some may experience a wide range of emotions; others may feel more shut down and depressed. The grieving process can take us into the depths of sadness and an inner emptiness that can feel overwhelming. The intensity and depth of our feelings may at times frighten us, and we may wonder if we can make it through the day or week and if we will ever feel like ourselves again.

It is essential to allow all of your feelings to surface, even the uncomfortable ones. For instance, many feel anger at their loved ones for passing over or for leaving before they had a chance to hear the words they longed to have them say. Some may feel angry at life or at God for the suffering that their loved one may have experienced. We may wonder if we did enough to take care of or help a loved one. We might be hard on ourselves for not visiting a loved one often enough while they were sick or before they passed over. Some tell me that they feel guilt for having an easy life, better health, or more positive experiences than a loved one who suffered.

Whatever you feel, let it surface. Your feelings don't hurt your loved ones on the other side or cause them pain or discomfort, and it doesn't create distance from them. Don't repress, deny, or pretend you feel fine when you don't. When we open our heart and feel our feelings, they begin to dissipate. The hold our difficult emotions have had on us loosens, and this allows our loved one's warmth and love to drift in and enter our heart. Shutting down or repressing our emotions can keep us from feeling a loved one's presence. Feeling the wide range of your emotions allows them to release and ultimately opens a channel for you to feel closer to your loved ones on the other side.

Along with difficult emotions, it is also important to feel the positive feelings you have for your loved one. Sometimes we don't allow ourselves to feel the tender and loving emotions, afraid that these feelings might make us feel worse and cause us to miss our loved one even more. In trying to protect ourselves we may unknowingly not allow ourselves to feel the joy and happiness that we continue to share with our loved one.

Our emotions are like the wind, clearing out the path and leading us to the calm and peaceful shores where our loved ones reside. Surrender to the grieving process, and it will guide you into their presence. As we feel and accept our emotions without judgment, we release them and make way for the higher vibrations of love to come through.

Our loved ones might also feel an acute sense of loss when they leave us; however, it is only temporary. Soon they are cradled in the powerful arms of the divine, among family and friends on the other side. Their heart opens and love pours in, healing the dark crevices of grief and filling them with a love that we can barely imagine. From this state of divine grace, our loved ones see and feel our suffering and long to lift our hearts into the love that they are now a part of.

Although we may want to receive a concrete thought message from those on the other side, it is often through feelings of love and comfort that they first contact us. Unfortunately, our grief can muffle and keep us from feeling their love.

The following emotional experiences may be signs that a loved one is close:

- A surprising sense of inner peace or spontaneous joy for no apparent reason.
- Feelings of heart-centered closeness accompanied by the awareness of the presence of a loved one on the other side.
- A sudden feeling of being forgiven and comforted for something that you did or didn't do in connection with a loved one on the other side.
- The heart awareness and comforting feeling that you are loved and adored.

EXERCISE
Heart-to-Heart Communication

To feel emotionally closer to a loved one on the other side, try this:

- Relax, breathe, and imagine your heart as a closed flower bud.
- As you breathe, visualize the petals of the flower opening one by one until the flower is in full blossom.
- Imagine an image of this flower is in your heart, open and receptive.
- Imagine a ray of sunlight extending from your heart flower to your loved one's heart.
- Feel the love that travels through this beam of sunlight from your loved one's heart to the flower within your heart.

- Imagine your heart flower absorbing the sunlight of love from your loved one.

Synchronicities and Signs

On the other side, our loved one's energy body looks a lot like the physical body. However, they are young, glowing, and at their best. The energy body is psychic and can do surprising things that might have mystified us in the physical realm. Yet, in the spirit realm these new abilities and talents are normal. For instance, our loved ones are able to see and feel those they left behind and know our thoughts. Through energy intentions they can transport themselves at will and appear in other locations and influence activities, people, and the natural world. Although they are not always able to fully comprehend and know how to manage these new abilities, other souls in the spirit realm teach and guide them.

Unfortunately, in the physical world we aren't always aware that our loved ones on the other side are now endowed with extraordinary abilities. Even though our loved ones are close and can see us, feel our emotions, and know our thoughts, feelings of loss and grief can cloud our intuitive receptivity. Those on the other side long to let us know that they are with us. They feel our concerns for them and want us to know that they are at peace and free of suffering.

Fortunately, the spirit realm is creative and clever and has provided another way for our loved ones to get our attention. Through utilizing signs, symbols, and synchronicities, our loved ones are able to break through the spirit-physical barrier and allow us a glimpse of their presence and love.

If our loved one's desire to let us know they are present is strong enough, they begin to experiment. Manipulating electrical currents is often one of the first signs our loved ones have success with. This includes such phenomena as flickering lights; turning lights on or off, including streetlights; setting off buzzers, alarms, and timers; stopping clocks or making them move ahead or behind; turning the television, phone, or computer off or on; or ringing phones. When my mother died, the speaker phone in my bedroom turned on, and the loud sound of a dial tone woke me up at 4:05 a.m. This was the exact time of her death.

Some loved ones send text messages and emails, and they may fool around on our computers. Of course, their emails and text messages aren't necessarily legible or signed by our loved one and are likely to appear to be random and nonsensical. Other common signs that loved ones place on our path are coins, feathers, or heart-shaped stones. They may also hide, move, or knock objects off a table or shelf.

Those on the other side often send us messages through the natural world, especially through birds. With their natural home in the skies, birds are often messengers between the heavens and the earth. Blue jays, cardinals, robins, and hawks tend to be the most common; however, the other side is able to send all varieties of birds our way. Another common companion of our loved ones are butterflies. They may appear soon after a loved one's passing, at a memorial service, or during anniversaries and special occasions. Along with birds and butterflies, our loved ones might also have a fox, deer, raccoon, or other animal cross our path. We might catch a sighting of a visitor from the natural world in our backyard, or a friendly squirrel might continually come to our window and seem to watch us from the ledge.

In their desire to let us know that they are close, our loved ones might also do their best to appear to us as an orb floating by in the air, or a camera might catch an orb or streak of light in a photo. Although it seems pretty near impossible, our loved ones can create a comforting image in a cloud or encourage a rainbow to form in the distant sky.

When we catch the fleeting scent of a loved one's perfume or another familiar fragrance, they are likely close. Our loved ones might call our name, appear to us in dreams, and create all kinds of synchronicities or unlikely coincidences that leave us spellbound.

The best way to know if a loved one is behind such phenomena as the bird who sits on your windowsill, or the dimes or pennies on your path, is to listen to your heart. There are no definitive characteristics within signs that will give the human-thinking part of us the complete confidence that a loved one sent it our way. Yet if your gut twinges, the hairs on your neck stand up to attention, or your heart opens with loving recognition, stop and listen. The best way to know if a sign is from your loved one, or what its meaning might be, is to listen within. Take a moment, be still, and open your heart. Hold on to the warm caress of love that comes your way or the inner thought or awareness that brings calm comfort. Don't let anyone, not even your own mind, take from you this union of souls across time and space.

Noticing and becoming aware of signs can assure us of our loved one's love and devotion. Some signs and synchronicities come our way simply to let us know that a loved one is close. A grandparent, parent, friend, or other loved one is checking in to say hello and bring a bit of heaven our way. However, there will also be times when we receive a sign and it feels as if a loved one is attempting to send us more of a message. These kinds of signs and synchronicities are invitations to further communicate with those on the other side. As messengers, they encourage us to take advantage of this opportunity to reach out and connect.

EXERCISE
Communicating with the Other Side Through Signs

When you notice a sign or synchronicity and feel led to reach out and further communicate with a loved one, try this:

- Following the observance of what feels to be a sign or synchronicity, find a comfortable and quiet place. This can be immediately after noticing a sign or even a few days later. Get into a relaxed position, close your eyes, and breathe long, deep cleansing breaths.

- Create an image in your inner mind of the sign that you received. It is not necessary to know who on the other side sent it. It is often more useful to simply imagine the sign and be open to the presence of whoever brought it your way. Send out a thought invitation to whoever this might be, letting them know that you would like to communicate.

- Continue to breathe long, deep breaths, exhaling any stress and tension, and become receptive.

- Try not to overly focus on logic or overthink. Open your heart and mind, continue to breathe and relax, and become receptive.

- Pay attention to your thoughts—not the linear thinking thoughts, but the more passive, observing-type thoughts. Notice the still small voice, the quiet murmurs and whispers, and the bits and pieces of any inner conversations that surface. If you suspect that you're receiving thought messages from a loved one on the other side, stay receptive and listen.

- You can also imagine an image of your loved one or say his or her name and project a thought or emotional message to them. Pause and become alert to any inner repetitive thoughts, words, or phrases that surface. They are often subtle and understated; however, they don't need to be loud or intense to be significant.

- Be aware of feelings of love, warmth, and comfort. Breathe into positive feelings and allow your heart to further expand. Opening our heart after losing a loved one may trigger any feelings of grief and sadness that have been buried deep in the heart to surface. The magnitude of love that the other side can shower on us has the capacity to dislodge any stuck emotions and wipe us clean. Receiving emotional intuitive energy from the other side can bring us comfort in times of loneliness and challenges and allows us to feel our eternal bond with the souls we love and cherish.

- If you experience sensations such as tingles of energy moving up your spine, the hairs on your arms or head standing up, or a warm or cool breeze moving by you, pay attention. These kinds of phenomena are a common signal that a loved one is close and that you're intuitively open and receptive. When we receive intuitive messages from the other side through our physical body, it is not always easy to logically decipher the meaning of the message. If you experience unexplained physical sensations, close your eyes, breathe, become receptive, and ask your loved one to send you a message in the form of thoughts or feelings. This simple intent will activate other receptive opportunities from your loved ones.

- When you notice a sign or synchronicity, it might appear as if the air surrounding it is luminous or brighter. Orbs or streaks and flashes of light also indicate the presence of a loved one. If you perceive these and other manifestations of light, close your eyes and relax. Allow any images to emerge. Even if they are partial images, fuzzy, or quick flashes, pay attention. Sometimes it will feel as if you are not "seeing" an image but knowing, feeling, or sensing it. Images might also be symbolic, figurative, or realistic, and might include seeing your loved one, who may or may not look exactly like they did in the physical life. Pay attention to the thoughts and feelings that accompany the sign or inner images.

- Don't expect to immediately understand the meaning of a sign or image, as it may take time to fully receive the message. Try not to overthink, and be patient. Eventually, the meaning, message, or sign from your loved one will easily sail into your consciousness when you least expect it.

Our loved ones are never far away and eventually become quite adept at sending us signs and messages. In my book *Sacred Signs & Symbols,* you can discover more information about how to better receive, understand, and communicate with a loved one through signs and messages.

———

In the next chapter you will begin to learn more about the purpose that you played in your loved one's evolution and growth and the role that they played in your life.

Section III

Transforming, Healing, and Evolving

Chapter 10

Lessons from the Soul Review

It is during the soul review that those on the other side become fully aware of the differing perspectives between the spirit realm and the physical world. Our loved ones' human failings are met with love, understanding, and forgiveness as they come to new awareness of the significance of what they have experienced during their physical life. The soul review can also offer insights and new perspectives on creating more positivity and joy in our everyday lives here on earth. As we incorporate lessons from the soul review, we feel closer to the loved ones on the other side.

Our soul is a mysterious, misunderstood part of us that rarely gets much of our conscious attention. However, when we pass over, it is our soul that remains. To say that death changes us is an understatement. When we pass over and enter the spirit realm, a new world opens up. Our soul-self recognizes this as home. All that we knew in the physical world is suddenly transformed, and as the illusions of the finite fall away, we come to see and know our true self. This self is more magnificent than anything that we have thought ourselves to be.

It is during the soul review that we make our transition from human rationale and consciousness to a more soul-based perception. Through the lens of this wise self, we review the challenges and opportunities we encountered in our physical lives. In this higher state of awareness, we become aware of the significance and impact that we had in others' lives and how others affected our life. Like a magnifying glass, we are able to clearly see, feel, and experience what we might not have been able to know about ourselves while in the physical realm.

In the spirit realm there are no failures. The choices and actions we took while in the physical life that led to love and kindness, as well as those that hampered our progress, are honored. On the other side, we are loving and wise, and we know that nothing can change this. In this enlightened state of awareness, we perceive the gifts and purpose that our loved ones brought into our lives. We discover that it is often with those whom we had a challenging relationship that we learn the most and make the biggest soul advancements. As we move through the soul review, our emotional wounds, pain, and suffering heal and become like a distant dream.

We don't have to wait until we pass over to reap some of the benefits of the soul review. Here in the physical world we can use it as a map through which we can be inspired to transform our perceptions and experience more joy. When we incorporate some of the soul review components such as forgiving ourselves and others, accepting that everything that we experience has a purpose, and choosing joy and positivity, we spiritually evolve.

Life on earth is a mixed bag of success and failure that sometimes seems unfair. However, there is no earthly or spiritual force that condemns us to a life of suffering or picks us out for special accolades and abundance. It is our own soul that creates both positive and difficult situations and experiences. Yet, we don't do this to reward or punish ourselves. Both challenges and good fortune can wake us to the power of our spirit and motivate us to act from its strength and wisdom. We come to this planet to progress along our evolutionary path and create and manifest what is in our heart and soul.

Choose to Love and Express Your Love

Being wealthy, popular, or famous in the physical world doesn't amount to much on the other side. In the physical life, we may have imagined that a life of unparalleled success or creating something that was noteworthy and admired by many was significant and important. We may have placed value on material things and outward accomplishments while minimizing the small acts that spring from our heart. On the other side we soon realize that the soul and the spirit realm have a different value system than the physical world.

During sessions, no one on the other side has ever mentioned any of their earthly accomplishments or material success. I don't know how much money they made or if they were admired or well-known. I've never had a spirit complain that in their earth life they were a victim of circumstances or treated unfairly. Whatever pride, self-importance, victimization, or pity we felt in the physical world drops away. Instead, it is the love that we have shared and given to others that is highly prized.

During the soul review we realize that love in the physical world is not only a feeling but an action and a choice. Those times when we selflessly put another's needs before our own, forgave another despite the pain they caused us, loved ourselves enough to walk away, or said no to what we had mistaken for love, are a source of joy and mastery.

We learn that all of our relationships are important and teach us about love. Some mirror the unconditional love of the heavens. Those that lead to confusion and the feeling that love has betrayed us or let us down motivate us to search within ourselves for the love we seek.

The soul review demonstrates that we have already achieved what we had been seeking in the physical world. We wake to the tremendous power of love that resides within us. Despite the challenges that we may have encountered in our relationships in our physical life, we become aware that perfect love has always been within and surrounding us, and we never had to search for it. We become aware that our feelings of unworthiness were a mask that kept us from recognizing who we truly are.

Even though our relationships here in the physical realm may often seem mundane and earthly, we are always cultivating a more mystical and soulful love. Despite what it may sometimes feel like, making the effort to love others and ourselves is a tremendous accomplishment. In our physical life it can be all too easy to find reasons to close our heart and not feel and express love for ourselves and others.

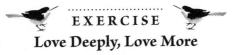

EXERCISE
Love Deeply, Love More

Keep putting in the effort to love, even when you don't want to. Eventually it will become natural and easier. You don't have to like everyone or everything that you and others do. Sometimes the most loving thing we can do is to walk away from a relationship with ourselves intact or say no to another and create boundaries. Love is not codependent and weak. Love is choosing to be present with our own and another's truth, knowing that sometimes they differ. Be free and be you, and support others in their freedom without judgment, control, or pity.

The kind of love that is essential is the love that springs from your soul. It's powerful and wise and always there for you to give and share.

Here is a simple exercise for the challenging times when love may seem far away or you don't feel worthy or able to give or receive:

- Become aware of when you don't feel loved or very loving toward others. Make the decision to allow love into your heart and to receive and share it with others.

- Take a few deep breaths and relaxing exhales. Release any inner tension and stress through long, deep inhales and clearing exhales. Make the intent to release whatever thoughts, beliefs, or feelings that seem to be blocking you from loving during the exhale.

- Keep breathing long, deep inhales and exhaling the stress, tension, and any blocks to loving through the breath. You don't need to fully understand and examine whatever beliefs, feelings, or thoughts surface, just imagine they can release through the exhale.

- As you begin to feel clearer, close your eyes and say aloud or to yourself, "Love is within me, and I'm calling it into my heart and total being to be felt and shared." Keep breathing long, deep breaths and repeat this statement.

- Keep breathing and opening your heart and allowing love in. Once you begin to feel the warmth of love, breathe into the heart and allow this love to expand within you. Love is powerful, and the blocks to loving will dissipate as you allow more love in.

- Imagine sending this love to a difficult or challenging situation that you are experiencing or to another person. Be sure to continue to breathe, call in this love, and allow it to move through you and ease any stress, tension, or emotional difficulties that you are experiencing.

See Your Life in a New Way

On the other side, we discover a new way to view and understand our earthly issues, circumstances, and ourselves. During my many years of giving readings, I've never communicated with anyone on the other side who held a grudge or was angry or disappointed with another or themselves. Instead, through the enlightened perspective and awareness that the soul review offers, we become aware that all we and others ever wanted was to be loved.

The significance and true meaning within even the smallest acts and decisions we made becomes obvious. We look in amazement, and sometimes shock, at what we held onto, felt was important, or devoted our energy to in the physical world. This shift into a more enlightened understanding of ourselves and life happens instantaneously and naturally.

When I share the messages that my clients' loved ones on the other side have for them, I'm often met with a perplexed look. People are often surprised by their renewed perspectives and insights. It may be hard to believe that when your grouchy grandfather or absentee or abusive parent passed into the spirit realm they became aware of and experienced how their actions and attitude affected you and others. They are not only humbled by this new awareness, they are ready to make amends.

Once we pass over we have no choice but to reevaluate our earthly lives. Through compassionate non-judgment, the spirit realm strips away our denial and excuses. The choices, beliefs, and actions of our earth life come back to us to be felt, forgiven, loved, and celebrated. Emotions like fear, stress, anger, and negativity are a faint memory. We know that they exist, but the high vibration of love doesn't support lower, ego-based emotions.

When we are reminded of these emotions during the soul review, we become aware of how they robbed us of joy. We may wonder why we allowed ourselves to dwell on and generate thoughts and feelings that only brought us suffering. With support from wise spirit beings, we learn that in the physical life our emotions were messengers. Like a spiritual compass, they informed us of when we were aligned with our soul and alerted us as to what would bring us pain and suffering. We perceive how feeling good attracted goodness into our lives, while fear and negativity brought more disappointment.

As we move through the review, the emotional patterns that kept us stuck and unable to experience more positivity and love transform. Our hearts open, and we realize that love was the most essential gift that we could give to ourselves and others.

For instance, neither Cindy nor her sister Karen had ever had a medium reading. With coffee in hand, they came in for a session on a cool October morning. I began the session with a prayer, and before I finished it, I felt the presence of their mother.

She was easy to communicate with and promptly let Cindy know that her suspicions were correct.

"Your mother says that she is flickering the lights in the kitchen. She also shows me what looks like a bird coming into the house. I see an image of her laughing; she loves surprising you. She says she doesn't mean to scare you, but your reactions are funny."

Cindy laughed and said, "Good, now I don't feel so crazy for talking to my oven. That darn light has been going off and on over and over since she passed, and I knew that bird had something to do with her. I don't know how it got in the house. I heard a bird chirping and saw a little sparrow sitting on my ceiling fan. I know Mom's been trying to get my attention … Is she upset with us?"

With this question, Cindy suddenly seemed tense and looked a bit apprehensive. However, her mother on the other side greeted the question with a calm peacefulness.

"Your mom is showing me a house. I get the impression this is her house and that it's been in the family for a long time. It looks empty… She says she's fine with the decisions you made about the house. She laughs and says she doesn't need it anymore."

"Really, she's not upset? That doesn't sound like her. Her house has been in the family for generations. She was born and raised there."

"Your mom shows me another house and now another one. It feels like these might be both of your homes. However, I get the feeling from her that she wanted one of you to live in her house."

"Yes, she did. It was important to her that one of us live there. It's where she grew up, and the house has been in the family for several generations. But we couldn't make it work. We both have kids and didn't want to move and have them change schools. We know we didn't fulfill her wishes and hope that she forgives us. That's why we're here; we don't want her to be mad at us."

"Your mother wants you to know that she didn't realize how controlling she was and the impact it had on both of you. 'The council helped me,' she says."

"What council? What is she talking about? I'm glad she's getting help, but I'm not sure what she's referring to."

"Your mom says that's what she calls the light beings that are helping her. She says that they are loving and know everything, even things she doesn't really care to know or remember. She didn't realize that she was so difficult. Your mom is smiling, and I can feel how proud she is of you for not moving into her house. She shows me a male, feels like a friend that bought the house. She says you need the money more than an old run-down house."

"We've felt guilty for letting one of her neighbors buy her home. He gave us a good price, and we know he'll take good care of it. It was hard to say no. I'm gonna sleep so much better knowing that she's at peace and being watched over," Cindy said.

EXERCISE
Creating a Heavenly Perspective

When an issue, problem, or challenge has you overthinking, stressed, or grouchy, try this:

- Write down the issue or problem that has you concerned or frustrated. Allow the emotions and thoughts surrounding this issue to surface.
- Take a deep breath and exhale any stress and tension. Continue to breathe long, deep relaxing breaths until you feel more centered and calm.
- Imagine that there is another way of looking at this issue. You may not know what it is, but allow yourself to take in the possibility.
- Tell yourself that your current beliefs and perspective is just one way of looking at your situation. Invite the idea that there may be another way to view what is happening that feels better.
- Close your eyes, breathe long, deep cleansing breaths, and ask for a loved one on the other side to help you perceive this issue differently. As you continue to breathe and relax, let go of any frustration, pain, or stress that you feel.
- Imagine that you are going through your soul review and the memory of this situation surfaces. What would you like to be feeling? From the perspective of eternity, what is important in this situation? What happens when an all-encompassing love and forgiveness is present?
- Keep breathing and allow yourself to receive any new feelings, thoughts, insights, or awareness.

- Imagine a higher force of love surrounding you and your situation. Feel the positive vibrations and allow your perspective to transform.

Forgive Quickly

Forgiveness is a major component of the life review. As we weave through our past experiences, we become more aware of the emotional impact of our choices, actions, and decisions, and new awareness surfaces. We have insight into how we impacted others in ways that we may not have realized at the time. With this new understanding, we seek resolution and have a sincere desire to apologize to those we may have hurt or harmed in any way. Forgiveness freely moves through us, and we let go of pain and resentments and better understand the significance of our earthly experiences. We feel the value of our differences with others and honor the individuality of all souls, even those we did not get along with and those who may have caused us pain or suffering.

In the physical life, it can be difficult to forgive someone or ourselves when we have been betrayed, hurt, abandoned, or treated unfairly. We hold onto the wrongs that we have endured and want whoever is responsible for our suffering to admit their guilt and feel the pain they caused us. All too often we may feel as if forgiveness may be a free pass that discounts and negates what we have experienced. On the human level, forgiveness can be a struggle that we're not always able to achieve.

During the soul review, forgiveness is easy. We don't hold onto the past and actions of another. Forgiveness flows like a river, delighting us with good feelings and light giddiness. Like love, forgiveness is within us as part of our eternal soul nature. When we forgive, we are released into a higher form of love that elevates our consciousness. Forgiveness is one of the most spiritual acts that we can practice. It allows our spirit to emerge and frees us and others.

Those on the other side often seek forgiveness for even small indiscretions. We experience more harmony and joy when we are forgiven and when we forgive others. We want to continue to feel the good feelings that forgiveness fills us with. If you ever intuitively get the sense that a loved one is close and asking for forgiveness, I hope you allow yourself and them this gift. Forgiveness releases old patterns and negative karma and restores and uplifts you and your relationship to one of love and grace.

Nettie learned that there is power in forgiveness, even in small things. When she came in for a reading, she looked around my office and slowly sat down, almost as if she was looking for spirits who might be lurking in the shadows and corners. Dressed in dark colors and with a sad look on her face, she appeared to be in mourning. Before I began the reading, I noticed a middle-aged, dark-haired male spirit standing behind her who I knew was her husband. I felt him pushing me a bit to get started.

"Your husband is here. He came in with you and wants you to know he's close…Not just now, he's with you quite a bit," I said.

Nettie's husband then spoke of his passing, shared memories, and gave messages about their children and grandchildren. About halfway into the session, I felt his emotional energy change. Instead of the outgoing and confident presence that made him easy to communicate with, he pulled back a bit.

"Your husband just shifted…It seems like he wants to say something, but he's hesitant…He's apologizing; he says that he took you for granted. I see an image of him sitting in front of what looks like a television and you're bringing him something, maybe a snack or a drink."

"Oh gosh, that's such a little thing, I loved doing what I could to make him more comfortable. Tell him there is no need to apologize," Nettie said.

"He says, it's more than this…Now he shows me an image that looks like him in his younger years…He feels ambitious and focused on his work. He tells me that work was all consuming…He says you gave up so much and he never thanked you."

"We met in law school. I had big dreams for my future as an attorney. We married soon after graduation, and I landed a good job in a corporate firm. It took a little longer for my husband. Eventually, he got a position in a private firm."

"You left your job, didn't you? As you're talking, your husband is showing me an image of you at home. He says he knew that you were bored, but he was glad that you quit your job," I said.

"That's true, when we decided to start a family, I left my job. I could tell that he was uncomfortable with my success. We never talked about it, but once I no longer worked, he seemed happier, and he liked me doting on him. Whenever I mentioned going back to work, he seemed sullen and I stopped bringing it up. In the end I know it was my choice to not go back to work. I don't blame him," Nettie said.

"Your husband knows that you sacrificed your dreams for him and that he didn't support you the way you did him. I can feel his heart opening when he shares this. I wish I could help you to feel the love and gratitude he is sending your way," I said.

"It's funny, last night I woke up, couldn't sleep, and felt my husband next to me. It felt as if he could really see me, not just as his wife, but a deeper me. I had a memory of him working on a big case. It was an important one and he spent late nights in his office for a few weeks. On the morning of the case, he left early and rushed out the door without saying goodbye. I remembered him shutting the door as I sat at the table staring into my coffee cup. For a moment I felt forgotten and cheated out of my profession. Anyway, as I remembered this last night, it felt like my husband knew what I went through and was apologizing to me. I don't know why, but I felt peaceful and loved and went back to sleep with no problem."

Forgiving Those on the Other Side

When you forgive someone, you are freeing yourself. What binds us to another is our unresolved past wounds and pain. We continually repeat dysfunctional emotional patterns until we heal and learn how to love and forgive ourselves and others.

It is not always easy to open ourselves to someone who has hurt or betrayed us. It can be even more difficult, at times, to trust and open ourselves to someone on the other side who has caused us pain. Their presence is intangible, and some may feel as if they have no guarantee that they are safe. Life can be challenging enough without the thought of being criticized or unloved by someone on the other side.

Sometimes people fear that forgiving another on the other side may mean that this spirit now has the ability to invade their space and create havoc. However, forgiving another does not mean that they are able to draw close to you from the spirit realm or influence you in any way. If you desire their presence, they're able to be with you. Otherwise, you have dominion over who comes close. No one can intrude and come close if you don't want them to.

It is always in our best interest to open our heart, forgive, and trust in the greater power of healing love. Even if we have no proof that someone has changed and is now aware of the pain they may have caused, you will heal and feel more whole as you let go of the past. Ask within for the strength to move forward and always be alert to the restorative and healing love that moves from the spirit realm into your heart.

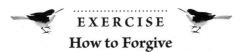

EXERCISE
How to Forgive

Forgiveness is a spiritual act and is not as personal as it may seem. When we forgive another, we step into a higher spiritual awareness that unbinds us from the burden of resentment and anger.

Make the simple intent to forgive another.

Resist the inner feeling or voice that tells you such things as you are allowing someone to get away with something. Or that forgiveness makes you weak and that it doesn't erase the pain.

Imagine an image of the person that you are ready to forgive. Tell them that you forgive them, and you are letting go of the pain. Let them know that it is no longer yours to carry. Take a deep breath and release whatever hurt and pain you've been carrying.

Tell yourself that you are ready to move forward in your life. The pain you have felt is no longer who you are. You are light and freedom; love and joy are waiting for you.

Flow with Your Emotions

During the soul review we shed our earthly emotions by fully feeling and letting them go. Through experiencing what others felt as a result of our actions, attitudes, and beliefs, we transform. All our emotions are accepted, and we are not shamed, blamed, or punished for them. The heaviness of negativity, fear, and guilt falls away.

In the physical life we experience a wide range of emotions in the span of any given day. We may feel happy, excited, sad, overwhelmed, depressed, satisfied, and many other emotions. While positive emotions help us to feel light and open, negative emotions can make us feel lethargic, heavy, or burdened. When our emotions are uncomfortable, we might repress or stuff them down or act on them in self-defeating and negative ways. We might try to avoid them by overthinking or acting out with addictive behavior or substances. At times we can project our repressed emotions onto someone or something else. It can sometimes feel as if we are ruled and controlled by our emotions and we're unable to let go and be in the present time. However, the soul review offers us some helpful tips as to how to feel our emotions, let them go, and transform.

EXERCISE
Breathe, Feel, and Release

On a daily basis, remind yourself to feel whatever you feel, as difficult as this may be.

Commit to letting go of your emotions and notice when you may be repressing them. Take a deep breath, feel whatever you are feeling, and then release the feelings through your exhale. Continue to breathe deeply, feel, and exhale.

If you find yourself overthinking and going back over a conversation or situation and replaying it, get in touch with your feelings, breathe, feel, and release. The core of obsessive thoughts and anxiety is repressed feelings.

If you are experiencing problems in a relationship, don't worry about who's at fault or what another could have or should have said or done. We all make mistakes. Let it go and continue to breathe and feel.

If you find yourself reaching for food, a drink, or something else that will stuff your feelings down, breathe and feel and release.

Whatever is happening, feel your feelings. If you are having a hard time letting them go, think of what you can do differently next time. Commit to a future positive action or practice, such as making better boundaries with another, speaking your truth, taking care of yourself, or breathing before you respond with anger.

When you feel as if you have released unsatisfying and difficult emotions, ask yourself what you would like to be feeling. Invoke a positive memory or thought that supports what you would like to feel. Breathe, feel, and absorb the good feelings.

Pay attention to feelings of ease, relief, and inner calm that come when you feel positive emotions. Focus on thoughts that support the feelings you want to be experiencing.

When we feel our emotions and let them go, we discover that not only does our power and freedom come back to us, forgiving ourselves and others feels good.

Live in the Now

During the soul review we are released from the past and any pain, hurt, confusion, or limited beliefs that we have held onto. We live in the now, in present time. The past has no influence on us and doesn't exist. There are no beginnings or endings, just cycles of energy, evolution, and creative activity.

In the physical world, we tend to stress and worry about the future. We plan and do our best to control what we want to experience and what comes our way. Our sense of who we are and what we are capable of is all too often overly influenced by our past. The environment that we grew up in, socioeconomic conditions, and the beliefs and opinions of our family and friends all too often define our potential and possibilities.

In the spirit realm, we come into the awareness that we are soul and spirit. We are not what we look like, what we experience, or what others have told us about ourselves. The divine is our mirror and reflects who we are. There is no past or future, and we live as pure creative beings.

In the physical life, we can live in this kind of freedom. We can free ourselves from the accumulated baggage of who we have thought ourselves to be. Similar to the soul review, this begins in allowing past repressed beliefs and emotions to surface, feeling them, and letting them go. This allows us to live in the present.

Sometimes the beliefs and emotions that unconsciously define our sense of self involve a loved one on the other side. If you have unresolved emotions with someone who now resides in the spirit realm, know that they are aware of the disharmony and seek healing with you.

Every so often in a session, an unexpected spirit shows up that my client is reluctant to communicate with. Usually this is a parent, sibling, grandparent, ex-spouse, or someone they had a falling out with or who hurt them. When I tell my client who is coming through, they often give me a look of dismay. Clearly, they are not excited that a spirit they may have had a difficult relationship with is present. However, there is always a purpose and reason why a particular spirit is present.

If my client is genuinely fearful or anxious, I let the spirit know they are not ready to be in their presence. If there is some interest in hearing from this soul, I encourage my client to allow them to come through.

In Kara's reading, this is what happened. When Kara came in the morning of our session, she seemed a bit distant and cautious. After saying a short prayer, I began the reading, which mostly focused on her present life and concerns. With just a few minutes left of our session, I felt the presence of a man who seemed as if he really wanted to come in. When he told me that he was Kara's father, I was surprised that he had not come in sooner.

"There is a man here who says that he is your father."

"My father? Why is he here?"

"He's quiet but persistent. He says he knows that you probably don't want to hear from him... He wants to apologize and let you know that he's sorry."

"What does he look like? Are you sure this is my father?"

"I think so. He has gray hair, kind of wavy," I said. "He's about six feet or so with a slim, wiry build."

"Well, that sounds like him. I wasn't expecting him."

"Do you want me to continue?"

"I guess."

I turned my attention to Kara's father in spirit. All of a sudden he became quiet and seemed reluctant to share. After encouraging him, I felt a rush of sadness and regret.

"Your father just sent me a wave of sadness. He regrets the way he treated you. He's emotional and it's hard for him to put this into words... Your father says that he feels the pain he caused you and wants you to know that he feels it all... everything... all the sharp words and the mistreatment... his not being there for you. He feels the loneliness and the pain he inflicted on you..."

"It was bad," Kara said. "He was abusive and for some reason took it out on me more so than my brother. I left when I was seventeen; it wasn't easy being on my own. He never offered to help or tried to contact me."

"I get the impression your father was hospitalized before he passed over. He shows me an image of himself lying in a bed unconscious, and he thanks you for visiting him. He knows that you were there," I said.

"We didn't talk for many years. Then my brother called and told me that my father had a stroke and was in a coma. I went to see him, and he passed over soon after."

"Your father wants you to know that he's getting help … he's working at it. He says that he is sorry for all the pain that he caused you. I can feel his love for you. I hope you can feel it, too, or maybe when you are more ready, you'll feel it."

"This is all such a surprise; I don't know why, but I didn't expect my father to come in today," Kara said. "I guess I'm glad he did and acknowledged the pain he caused me. I need some time to process all of this."

About a year after our session, Kara contacted me for another session.

When she came in for our appointment, she was much more at ease than she'd been at our first session. As she got comfortable in her chair, she started to talk. "When my father came through in our last reading, I didn't know what to make of it. A few weeks later I started to have dreams about my childhood. Eventually I went to therapy and it helped me to process the past and let go of the pain. I'm close to forgiving my father; I'm almost there. It feels good to be able to let the resentment go. I feel freer and more open and present to all that life has to offer. The pain that was hidden within me for so long was controlling me more than I knew. Anyway, I met someone a few months ago and I'm starting a new job next week. I wanted to go over some of this with you."

EXERCISE
You Are Presence

The following exercise will help you become aware that you are a boundless and free spirit. As you let go of who you thought yourself to be, the powerful and internal you emerges.

Get into a comfortable position and close your eyes. Breathe long, deep cleansing breaths and relax. Continue to breathe and release any stress and tension through the exhale. As you breathe, allow any thoughts or emotions to surface and lovingly accept them. Then send them on their way through a cleansing exhale. Continue to clear your mind and heart in this way.

Open your heart and ask for a loved one or higher being from the spirit realm to be present. Continue to breathe and allow the calm and peaceful higher vibrations of the spirit realm to be with you. Imagine that everything that you experience is temporary and that it will all pass.

Open your heart and mind and take a long, deep breath. Feel your presence in your body. Then feel it expanding outside of your body.

Tell yourself, "I experience myself through my physical body, but I am not my body."

Take a long, deep breath and feel the emotions and feelings that move through you, one after another. Feel your emotions.

Tell yourself, "I experience myself through my emotions, but I am not my emotions."

Take a long, deep breath and become aware of your thoughts. Allow your thoughts to emerge one after another. Breathe and relax.

Tell yourself, "I experience myself through my thoughts, but I am not my thoughts."

Take a long, deep breath, relax, continue to breathe, and ask yourself, "If I am not my thoughts, emotions, and physical body, then who am I?"

Allow your soul essence to emerge. Continue to breathe and feel your presence: free, uncontainable, and without limit.

It is through our soul review that we become fully aware of who we are and who we have always been. Despite the issues, problems, and personality defects that we may have experienced here in the physical world, the truest part of us is whole and pure. When we pass over, we meet our loved ones who are already on the other side and the wise and loving guides and beings who have been guiding and loving us throughout our earth life. We also come face-to-face with the power of our own soul. It, too, has been guiding us and waiting for us to embrace and fully recognize who we truly are.

––––––

In the next chapter you'll learn more about what those on the other side can teach us about relationships.

Chapter 11

Relationship Challenges, Past Lives, and Soul Contracts

Love and relationships occupy a fair amount of our time and attention in the physical world. At any given time, we might be looking for a soulmate, trying to improve or understand a relationship, or healing from or contemplating what happened in a relationship. It may be that it is through love that we come the closest to experiencing our most soulful and loving self. Poets and contemplatives throughout the ages have attempted to capture and express the deep communion of love that exists between souls.

For all the focus that we put on relationships here in the physical world, it is difficult to fully know who we are and what we want. It can be even more puzzling to fully know another. In our relationships, even the most loving ones, we at times struggle to understand and get along with our partner, friends, and family. Bombarded with day-to-day challenges, activities, and a multitude of other issues, our awareness of self and others is too often confined to the mundane.

Here on earth we search for love and desire to feel connected and accepted by others. However, this is not so on the other side. The soul review demonstrates that we already embody the love that we had been seeking. We wake to the tremendous power of love that resides within and all around us. Its intelligence and wisdom guide us to heal our relationships and rest in the eternal greater love that never ceases. On the other side we realize that even though our relationships here in the physical realm may seem mundane and earthly, we have been cultivating a more mystical and soulful love all along.

For instance, when I began the reading with Julie, a single woman with two adult children, I could feel her apprehension. After giving her a few messages, a man came forward who felt like a husband.

"A taller man with a full head of gray hair and a stocky build is coming in. Do you have a husband on the other side? He shows me a wedding ring."

"Yes, that's Matt," Julie said.

"He's showing me his heart. I'm getting the impression that he died of a heart problem. I'm not sure why he keeps showing me his heart... He says that there was nothing else that could have been done. It was his time... Now he shows me a beach... It feels good... He feels happy here," I said.

Julie started to cry, and her husband, Matt, continued to talk.

"I'm getting an image from Matt. He's showing me the beach again. I'm getting the impression that he died there. He wants you to know that's where he wanted to pass over. It was peaceful for him."

"I made him go to the beach that weekend. We spent the night in our favorite hotel near the shore. He hadn't been feeling good. He was on heart medication and had a congestive heart illness. It was my fault he passed; I should not have talked him into going. I woke up and he was gone. He was next to me in bed when he passed, and I didn't even know it... Can he forgive me?"

"Your husband feels your remorse and guilt. He wants you to know that he was ready. He drifted off and his mother came for him. He felt no pain—he went over while asleep, never woke up. There is nothing to forgive; it was his time, he says... Your husband wants you to know that his love for you is all encompassing. He sees, feels, and knows you in a more soulful way and plans on romancing you from the other side. I'm not sure how he's going to do this, but he seems to be intent on loving you in a big way... He's showing me a rose, a red rose. Was there a rose that bloomed in your garden at an odd time of year?"

"Oh, wow, yes, a rose bloomed outside late winter. I saw it from my bedroom window and couldn't believe it. I had to go outside and check to make sure it was real. Was that Matt?"

"It appears that was Matt, and he's only just beginning, he says. Be on the lookout; there's more to come. He loves you."

Understanding Relationships Through a Spiritual Lens

Our soul always points us in the direction of positivity and love and encourages us to share and express this with others. Unfortunately, our human conditioning, fears, and self-focus often veer us in the opposite direction. Yet, even when we ignore the whispers of our soul, we never really fail. No matter how much our ego gets in the way of expressing and acting in loving ways in our earthly relationships, the soul is pure, whole, and powerfully loving. When we pass over, we discover this truth.

As we experience our earthly emotions during the soul review, we flow into a higher state of awareness. We become aware of the love that has always been within us. In the earth life we may have longed to be unconditionally loved, adored, and cared for. Unfortunately, in the human realm this kind of love doesn't always come easily. This is not true of our spirit life. On the other side, love is like the sun and air. It is a natural part of the environment and constantly nurtures us. There is no striving after love and no obstacles get in our way of receiving it.

In the loving peacefulness of the soul review, we view and feel our past interactions with family members and friends. As we connect with these memories, emotions and thoughts from the past surface. Simultaneously, new insights emerge that help us to better understand the lessons and deep love between ourselves and others.

On the other side, relationship issues and difficulties are nonexistent. Through the lens of our soul awareness we perceive the soul's grander purpose within our relationships, even those that were difficult in the physical life. The often-hidden significance is revealed, and we understand why some relationships in the physical realm were harmonious and why we experienced challenges in others. We become aware that success in relationships is not always measured by the commonly accepted standards of the physical world.

As we ponder and experience past memories, we become aware of the interconnectedness between ourselves and those we have been in relationship with. We realize that the things that we didn't like about another reflect aspects of who we are. Within our past judgments, rejection, and non-acceptance of others, we become aware that we have denied and repressed aspects of ourselves that are in need of love, acceptance, and healing.

This discovery invokes forgiveness, and love moves through and heals our soul. The guilt that we harbored transforms into insights and new awareness. The meaning and reasons why things happened the way that they did in the physical world begin to make sense. We become aware that despite the decisions and choices we might have agonized over, there was and is a higher order and a divine path that we have unknowingly been following. All along we have been led to those activities, people, and circumstances that supported our healing and soulful evolution.

As we embody and heal the discarded, unhealed aspects of self that we projected onto others, our separation from our higher self lessens. The differences between ourselves and others dissolve and feelings of love and joy easily flow. Long-standing emotional patterns that have negatively impacted previous generations also begin to heal.

Why We Choose Challenging Relationships

The healing and restoration we receive when we resolve an issue with another extends beyond the relationship with that particular person. This is true for the healing that takes place in our relationships in the physical world and those in the spirit realm as well. Our relationships are a mirror that reflects what needs love and healing within ourselves. It's never just about another person or an isolated problem. The issues or difficulties that we confront within relationships provide opportunities for healing and soul expansion.

Challenges in the physical world shake us out of our slumber and force us to become aware of what needs healing within us. Through the eyes of eternity, there are no victims. We each consent to whatever we experience and often choose difficulties as a fast track to soul growth. When we heal and improve our relationships with others, we also heal ourselves at a soul level. This changes the course of our future, as we cease attracting people and situations that mimic what inwardly needs our attention.

On the other side, we fully experience the truth that whatever we do to others, we do to ourselves. Through our selfless acts we experience more joy and love. I've never had anyone in spirit defend any of their behaviors in the physical world that caused another pain or suffering. Some may express how they didn't know any better and that they were motivated by fear, or they themselves were wounded or suffering. However, these are not excuses but insights into what led to unloving behavior. During readings, loved ones on the other side do their best to assure their earthly people that they were operating from fear, pain, and past negative beliefs.

For instance, Vera is the mother to two young children. Soon after we began our session, I felt the presence of Vera's mother. She was easy to connect with and shared messages and insights for the family she left behind. From the spirit realm she doted on her grandchildren and did her best to comfort and be present. We were almost finished with the session when her mother showed me a male next to her in the spirit realm that felt like her father.

"Your mother wants you to know that she is with her father," I said.

"Really? Are you sure? She barely knew her father," Vera said.

I turned back to her mother, but she was persistent. "Your mother says it's her father and they are working some things out. I get the impression that she was angry with him for most of her life. Your mother says that she better understands why everything happened the way that it did."

"I'm not sure what she means," Vera said.

"When I ask your mother to explain, she says that she chose her father knowing that he would not be present in her life. She says that not having a father helped her to be independent. One of her soul lessons was to learn how to be strong and take care of herself. Her father needed to learn a lesson too."

"What lesson was he learning? From what I know he didn't seem like a good father, maybe not even a good person," Vera said.

I turned back to her mother, wondering myself what lesson he could possibly be learning. However, instead of her mother, her grandfather came forward.

"Your grandfather is here. Is this okay with you?"

"Yes, I'd like to hear what he has to say. I never met him. He died before I was born, and I probably wouldn't have met him anyway."

"He says he's sorry for the pain he caused your mother. He knows how much this affected you growing up. He says that one of the lessons he learned is that you can never really walk away from anyone or anything. He thought he could escape the financial and emotional responsibilities that come with a wife and child. He didn't want to grow up but found out there is truly never an escape from anything. Throughout his life his heart ached because of his actions, and he shows me that he never forgot about what he did to your mother. It caused him pain throughout his life, but he was too proud to reach out and apologize. He says it only feels good to love. That's it, nothing else is satisfying. He had to learn the pain in selfishness," I said.

There is meaning and purpose within the relationship problems, issues, and challenges that we experience. When a loved one passes over, we may feel as if it is too late to resolve past misunderstandings and feel peace. However—no matter how your loved ones treated you, or whatever they did or didn't do that made you feel less than worthy—once in the spirit realm, they now are able to love you. From your loved ones' vantage point, they better understand why things happened the way that they did. If your loved ones were loving, supportive, kind, and devoted to you while in the physical world, their love is amplified tenfold.

Revelations of Other Lifetimes

Have you ever been drawn to someone and wondered why? Even though they may not have the kind of qualities that you usually find attractive, you are drawn to them and feel compelled to get to know them. Equally confusing, we might not always understand why we experience challenges with some and no matter how hard we try, we cannot feel the ease and compatibility we long for.

Our relationships can be a source of comfort, friendship, companionship, understanding, and deep feelings of love and connection. Relationships can also at times be confusing. Even those we dearly love and adore can frustrate, confound, and sometimes cause us pain. When a relationship isn't giving us what we had hoped, we may become frustrated and disappointed. This often leads to arguments, conflicts, and accusations, and we may give up or shut down. As we grow and evolve, we may learn how to better confront issues and work toward understanding our partner and ourselves, as well as finding resolution. Sooner or later we all learn that it is pretty much impossible to control another and a relationship. No matter how hard we try, relationships can sometimes seem to be confusing and have a purpose that we don't always understand.

On the other side, we know that our soul journey with loved ones doesn't end when we leave the physical life and that it doesn't begin in the physical life, either. During the soul review, we begin to perceive our relationships through the perspective of eternity. We recognize that our emotional patterns with others continually pull us back to the earth, life after life with the same souls, to evolve and heal.

As we become aware that we have lived other lives, we learn that we have experienced the same emotional patterns and challenging circumstances from one life to another. Although in previous earth lives we may have lived in other places and looked physically quite different from life to life, we feel familiar feelings and repeat the same kind of emotional issues and repetitive circumstances. The significance of what we experienced in the physical life, as well as the importance of the gifts we freely shared with others, is better understood.

Before we are born into the physical world, divine beings assist us in developing a "to-do" list or plan for our life. This soul plan includes the emotional patterns, challenges, lessons, and gifts that we come here to express and share with others. Masterfully woven together through time and space, the universe responds to our soul's requests and orchestrates a life of purpose and meaning.

Not only do we encounter similar patterns and circumstances, we also continually incarnate with the same souls over and over. Our husband or wife may have been our child, our mother may have been our grandmother, and our friend might have been a past lover in another life. Weaving in and out of one another's orbit from life to life, we become aware of the ways that we support others and perfect our ability to love and receive love from one another.

Our family members, romantic interests, friends, and even some of our casual acquaintances play a role in our soul's plan, and we serve a role in theirs. It is through our interactions with others that both our emotional wounds and our highest expressions of love come to light. Sometimes our most difficult and confusing relationships trigger our deeper soul issues, bringing to the surface what we need to heal and transform. Through our connection with others, we are often forced to examine our feelings, thoughts, and actions. In contrast, our harmonious and loving connections have the power to activate our higher soulful self. They allow us to remember that the uplifting essence of divine love is within us. In the best of our relationships, it can feel as if we experience a bit of heaven.

EXERCISE
Heal Past-Life Patterns

The dynamics that you are experiencing between yourself and another were set in motion very long ago. Quite often, past-life patterns have an intensity that doesn't always make sense given the present circumstances. For instance, we might not understand why we are profoundly drawn to another or why we feel compelled to keep trying to make a relationship work, even if it is difficult. We may be perplexed as to why certain people provoke powerful emotional responses over issues and problems that we normally don't get worked up over. Or we may wonder why communication and understanding with some is natural and easy and why we feel as if we are familiar with those who we may have just met.

If you experience confusing and intense emotional patterns with another, here are some suggestions:

- As tempting as it may be, don't blame another for what you are feeling and experiencing.
- Accept that even though it doesn't always appear this way, you attracted this person because there is something you need to heal, forgive, accept, share, express, or make peace with.
- Write down the situation with a focus on the emotions and feelings you are experiencing.
- As the intensity of the emotions begin to dissipate through writing and feeling, ask yourself, what within you needs love and healing?
- Close your eyes, relax, breathe, and listen within. Ask for a loved one on the other side, your angels, or a divine source to be present. Allow yourself to receive love and healing.
- Become receptive, continue to listen within, and become aware of new awareness, guidance, and insights.
- Ask within if there is any action that you need to take to heal the emotional pattern. Sometimes what we receive goes counter to what we believe we want. For instance, to heal and resolve past-life patterns we might need to walk away from a relationship, take back our power, pursue heal-

ing of our emotional wounds, forgive ourselves or another, transform low self-esteem, or let go of expectations for ourselves or another.

• Because past-life patterns can be deeply ingrained and affect our lives in a multitude of ways, it might be necessary to seek professional counseling or healing.

You can only heal your part in a past-life connection with another. When you do, you free yourself from the pattern. Even if the other person involved has not done their part, you are released into a higher vibration of creative freedom. Sometimes it can be difficult to let go and allow another to heal in their own time and space. Remember, you can only do your part, and self-healing is the most powerful thing you can do to inspire healing in another.

Loved Ones and Our Soul Group

A soul group is a collection of souls who evolve and grow together and whose bond is rooted in divine love and the higher plan of creation. Our family and friends are often a part of our soul group, and we continually incarnate with these familiar souls. Weaving in and out of different lifetimes with one another, we play an important role in one another's healing, growth, and evolution. In the physical life our family members often have differing viewpoints, beliefs, and attitudes. This contrast between how we see things and another's viewpoint provides us the opportunity to become more aware of what speaks to our personal truth.

For instance, some family members may trigger aspects of our nature that are unconscious and need to come to the surface for healing and transformation. At times, we disagree with the behavior and beliefs of some of our family members. Even though this can be confusing and disappointing, this provides a contrast that helps us become more aware of who we are and what is important to us. Our differences with others can also help us to develop more adaptability, empathy, and compassion.

Quite often we don't feel as spiritually aligned and connected to our family members as we would like to be. However, they are an integral part of our journey both in the physical and spiritual worlds, even when their beliefs and views are quite different from ours. They spur on our growth and consciousness expansion through a kind of soul friction.

Although most souls continually incarnate with the same soul group of family and friends, there are some who choose to enter into a certain family in order to help it evolve and heal. This usually happens when a family pattern has become so destructive and negative it is nearly impossible for one family member to create change. A higher-evolved soul may then incarnate within the family to break through the energetic deadlock.

From early childhood these evolved souls are usually perceived as different by the other family members. They may be more sensitive, insightful, confident, and independent. Unfortunately, their differences are not always accepted and admired, and they might become the family scapegoat and be blamed and ridiculed. Equally as common, they become a family's source of pride, as they are able to thrive and achieve what others have not been able to. Their life choices are generally free of the self-defeating and soul-crushing patterns that have hindered generations. For example, in a family that has ingrained addiction issues, this family member has no craving or desire for mind-altering substances. In a family that has suffered a genetic debilitating illness, a higher-evolved soul may enter the family and heal the DNA by introducing a resistant strand. Sometimes this evolved soul helps the family by example and by introducing new gifts and talents into the family patterns.

On the other side, our awareness and connection with our family and friends continues to evolve. The souls that we shared our physical lives with are close, and we love them in a more soulful and expansive way than we did in the physical world. Without the ego and the fears and expectations that often get in the way of fully loving, we experience their beauty and individuality. Where once there may have been control issues or misunderstandings, love is now the vast and open freedom through which we experience one another.

Our Soul Contracts

Before coming into the physical life, we form a soul agreement or contract with other souls. In these soul contracts we agree to play a specific, supportive, and loving role in their life, and they agree to the same in our life. We become aware of the challenges and experiences that our soul would like to create in the soon-to-be-physical life. We also become aware of the soul needs and desires of the earth family members, friends, and acquaintances that we will incarnate with. The mysterious and yet precise universe then spins its magic. A life path map is created through which our needs and desires, and those of our earth soul group, overlap, converge, and intersect with one another. Throughout our life we encounter these souls who we have mutual agreements with. We may support, challenge, teach, share unconditional love, and experience joy with one another. We might also trigger one another's unconscious wounds and motivate each other to move through challenging beliefs and issues.

Once we pass over into the spirit realm, these soul agreements are included as part of our soul review. We become aware of where and how we progressed on our path and when we verged away from it or became stagnant. Our commitment and dedication to our growth, as well as our commitment to the role that we agreed to play in others' lives, is honored and recognized.

During the soul review, we become aware of our soul contracts with those we were in relationship with and begin to more fully understand why things happened the way that they did. Tension, conflict, and other confusing patterns are unraveled, and the greater purpose behind what may have seemed problematic is revealed. Through this process we come into our natural soulful state of complete love and peace.

Once in the spirit realm, the soul contracts we shared with our loved ones who are still in the physical world evolve. Instead of some of the earthly challenging aspects of relationships, our soul contracts are now focused on love, healing, and devotion. For instance, the soul contracts that we share with our spouse, children, grandchildren and friends still in the physical body are still in operation but shift to that of providing unconditional love, guidance, comfort, and healing.

Clients sometimes worry that once a loved one has passed over they may incarnate or move on to new celestial experiences and forget about them. This is never the case. Your parents, children, siblings, and other relatives and friends in the spirit realm are still as you remember them, only better, more loving, and wiser. We don't incarnate into another life on earth until the loved ones that we knew and were together with in the physical world pass over. We then create another soul contract with these familiar souls for a future life together. Until then, our loved ones on the other side remain as we remember them for several earthly generations. However, there are a few exceptions. When a child passes over at a young age, they may choose to incarnate back into the earth life more quickly. When this is the case, they normally come back into the same family. If this is not possible, they incarnate into the family of an extended family member. There are also souls who complete their earth life experiences and don't have to come back. Still, some may choose to reenter the physical life to help, serve, and advance other souls.

Relationship Advice from the Soul Review

We are born into the physical life with a bit of amnesia. We can't remember where we came from, what is important, and the deep beauty of our soul and others'. Unlike the spirit realm, we also don't have the benefit of clear insight into the subtle purpose and soulful essence often hidden within our relationships. We muddle through and do our best to support and provide those we love with all they need to thrive. However, issues and problems inevitably surface. Although we may not fully know the significance of our relationship struggles and day-to-day circumstances, the soul review offers us a few pointers to help us on our way:

- Trust that every relationship has a purpose.
- Accept that you may not know the deeper purpose within a relationship, and this is okay.
- Remind yourself that there are no accidents or random happenings. It's not only about what life brings your way; it's how you perceive and grow from it that counts.
- Trust that whoever shows up in your life has a gift for you. It may not be what your conscious self wants and hopes for, but your soul welcomes it.
- Challenges and issues will arise, and no one is to blame. You can learn and evolve from whatever you are experiencing and whoever you are in relationship with.
- Remember that every issue or problem that you encounter with another has its roots within you. There are no victims. What you see in another is a reflection of a hidden aspect within you.
- Listen within and allow your often unconscious emotional patterns and pain to surface. Get help if you need it. Work with a therapist, counselor, or healer to release, let go of, heal, and transform trauma, past abuse, limited beliefs, and old wounds. Your relationships will improve.

• Know that you are healing, evolving, and fulfilling your purpose. Once you release and heal old wounds and limiting beliefs and feelings, you are free and you change your future for the better.

Your loved ones on the other side can help you to evolve and move beyond unsatisfying and sabotaging emotional patterns that show up in your relationships. Those who reside in the beauty and wonder of the spirit realms have no ego needs and no desire other than to love and support you. Even family members you did not necessarily get along with in the physical life send you the silent but potent message that you are loved, forgiven, cherished, and adored.

———

In the next chapter you'll have the opportunity to become aware of the purpose and gifts within your relationships with those on the other side.

Chapter 12

A Mini Soul Review

Every relationship has a unique story that has been woven and intertwined over many lifetimes. However, from the earthly perspective we are not always aware of the inherent soulful meaning and significance of what we are experiencing in our relationships with our family, friends, and acquaintances.

If you are wondering what your soul purpose may be, look to your relationships and the recurring emotional themes throughout your life. What draws us back to the earth over and over are our emotional patterns. The love within us needs to match the love of the heavens; otherwise, we get pulled back into the physical world.

Everyone who comes into our life embodies an essential and beneficial something that we need. In the same way, we have a gift for others. Of course, we are rarely fully aware of what this special something is. However, little clues surface that hint at the grander scheme of things.

For instance, in some of our relationships it is easy to give and receive love. Something clicks and we don't have to work to understand one another. We feel joy and a sense of connection. With others we may experience more confusion and misunderstandings. A relationship may trigger the unhealed and unconscious beliefs and wounds that we carry from life to life, forcing us to acknowledge and heal them.

It is through our connection with others that we have the opportunity to engage in our soul's purpose and evolve. While we all have unique emotional patterns, there are common lessons that we have all come here to experience.

Our earthly relationships teach us such things as how to take back our power, forgive ourselves and others, and practice devoted commitment. To become more self-aware and let our authentic self shine through, we learn how to say no when we mean no and say yes when we mean yes. We might also need to learn how to let go of relationships that don't support our highest good and walk away from negativity or abusive situations. In addition, through our example, others may learn how to practice such things as how to be vulnerable and intimate, listen to and support others, be selfless, speak their truth, and experience joy. The common thread running through all our relationships is to love fully, allow others the freedom to be themselves, heal our wounds and character flaws, and develop and express kindness and compassion.

At the same time, it is not necessary to be perfect. At times we will be selfish, give away our power, suppress our truth, not express love, and generally score low on the love meter. It's okay when we make a mistake. There is no punishment or shame for being human. We are a work in progress, and we do the best that we can at the time.

Kenni Shares Our Purpose

During the soul review, we learn that every attempt we make to move beyond our stunted emotional patterns and love ourselves and others is significant. Even the small acts that don't seem to amount to much heighten our love vibration. Every relationship serves us in some way. Even those that make us want to pull our hair out or run the other way come into our life for a reason. However, it's not always obvious what purpose our soul has in mind when someone comes into our life.

For instance, after my ex-husband, Kenni, passed over, it took me several years to understand the purpose of our relationship. I knew in my heart that there was a reason and purpose in our time together, I just wasn't sure what it was. It wasn't until after his physical death that I became fully aware of all that he taught and gave me.

During one of Kenni's visits from the spirit realm, he apologized for not doing more to save himself from the grip of addictions. He wanted me to know that there was nothing I could have done differently that would have made a difference in his choices. When he went back to playing music full-time, his drinking increased and he started to use drugs. This was his choice, he told me. Once on the road playing in clubs and touring with bands, he went back to a lifestyle he had been trying to escape.

"I had an addiction issue," he said. "I wanted that lifestyle, as destructive as it was, and I knew you would never be comfortable with it. There was nothing you could have done to change this, nothing anyone could have done."

Although I knew that his drinking and drug use were his decision, Kenni taking responsibility for his actions relieved the lingering thought that maybe there was something I could have done that would have changed the outcome.

Early one morning, he came to me while I lay in bed half awake. His voice was gentle but to the point.

"I've learned that we came together in part for a shared lesson. I was given the opportunity to love in a simple and pure way, the way I always wanted. But I needed an escape and couldn't do it. I've also discovered that my addictions offered you an opportunity to heal and learn. I guess I triggered some of the wounds you had from your father's drinking. My guides say that you agreed to this experience as well."

Somewhere in the recesses of my consciousness, I knew that marrying a man with an addiction issue was no accident. When I was six years old my father left, and I never understood why. However, I did know that he would have rather been drinking whiskey at the local bar with his friends than being with his children. Still, when he walked out, I took it personally and didn't recognize the role drinking played in his behavior.

Kenni's drinking brought up some of the confusion and pain I felt as a child. Witnessing the changes in Kenni's behavior and personality as his drinking increased and then morphed into drug use helped me to better understand the nature of addictions and my powerlessness. In this life, which has been devoted to helping others, I needed to learn that I cannot change anyone and I'm not responsible for anyone else's behavior. While we can support and love another, we change when we are ready.

Taking Back Our Power with Help from the Other Side

When a loved one passes over it may feel as if it is too late to clear up misunderstandings, heal a wound, or ask for forgiveness. However, it is never too late.

Sometimes the work that we cannot do here with another happens effortlessly when they are in the spirit realm.

Even though healing doesn't take place in the physical world, it is no less real and essential when it occurs after someone passes over. Our love, forgiveness, and compassion can have a profound effect on our loved ones on the other side, and they in turn exert a positive influence on us. The healing we experience with our loved ones on the other side seeps into every aspect of our lives, enriching all that we experience, and creating miracles.

During the soul review, our loved ones on the other side accept their role in creating the circumstances of their earthly life and take responsibility for their choices and actions. Those things that they consciously and unconsciously attracted are examined, and hidden motives, beliefs, and wounds are uncovered. It is through this process that they release whatever is not aligned with their highest good and experience heightened levels of love, bliss, and joy.

Our loved ones on the other side are transforming through enlightened awareness and unconditional love, and we can too. Sometimes a family member or friend passes over before we are able to resolve an issue or past hurt. When we mourn someone who left before we were able to heal the relationship or receive the kind of love and connection with them that we had hoped for, it can be especially difficult. We mourn not only our loss, but the loss of what will never be. We may feel stuck in a painful past and unable to move forward.

When we hold onto the hurt, bitterness, and resentment of past relationships, we hurt ourselves. This pain can linger in our body, causing us mental, emotional, and physical issues and illness. We are also likely to repeat the unresolved issues in other relationships.

The thought of connecting and healing a relationship with someone on the other side may seem unattainable and overreaching. Opening ourselves to the unknown can take us out of our comfort zone, and reaching out to someone who has caused us pain can be even more daunting.

However, we are closer to those on the other side than what we may think. Your loved ones are with you and encourage your healing and continued growth. Your attempts to reach out will always be met with love. It's not possible to hold on to resentment, pain, anger, or any emotionally toxic energy in the spirit realm. Once we pass out of the physical body, we are released from the grip of the limited and negative emotions and beliefs of the physical world. As our loved ones go through the soul review, their love becomes purer, selfless, and compassionate. The earthly patterns that may have kept us bound to unhealthy and less-than-satisfying love relationships fall away. The problems, issues, wounds, and painful experiences our loved ones encountered in the physical world are healed and transformed. The emotional patterns that may have created obstacles to intimacy and brought pain or motivated them to hurt others are understood through enlightened awareness.

During the soul review, unsatisfying ways of relating, and the repetitive and unconscious emotional beliefs that have brought us more pain than pleasure, are understood from the higher perspective of the soul. If we experienced unloving or unhappy relationships, we uncover the reasons why. We examine what we created in the physical world and learn that we cannot solely blame others for what we have experienced in our relationships. Even in cases where we have been mistreated or neglected, we become aware of how unconscious feelings and beliefs, such as a sense of unworthiness or a lack of self-love, contributed to our experience.

Becoming aware of how we unknowingly attracted difficulties doesn't mean that those who abuse, harm, or hurt others are not responsible for their behavior. No one comes into life to suffer and be abused. Those who knowingly inflict harm go through a kind of spiritual rehabilitation on the other side where they feel and become aware of the pain they caused others. However, this isn't a punishment, but an opportunity to develop empathy, forgiveness, and compassion. Ultimately, we learn that what we do to others, we do to ourselves.

During the soul review we let go of negativity, heal old wounds and limited beliefs, and learn how to live in more love and joy. The sheer force and magnitude of divine love breaks down our barriers and we live as our soulful highest self.

Here on earth we can do a mini version of the soul review and experience healing and increased awareness. Although we aren't able to fully immerse ourselves in the blissful energy of the other side, we can still receive its benefits.

EXERCISE
At Peace with Those on the Other Side

This exercise will assist you in healing a relationship wound, pattern, or issue with someone on the other side. Our loved ones, even those who were less than loving in the physical world, love and receive love without restraint. They are eager to send love our way and help us heal.

To begin, think of someone on the other side who you would like to feel a sense of peace and completion with. This can be someone who may have passed over before you resolved an issue or problem. Even if you experienced an overall positive and loving relationship, there may be something even in a good relationship that you would like to heal. In addition, you can also heal and clear energy with a relative or ancestor that you didn't know or someone who you knew just briefly whose influence on the family or a particular family member is significant.

Once you have decided who you would like to connect with, take a few deep, long breaths and relax. Then become aware of an issue, recurring pattern, or problem in the relationship that you would like to resolve and heal. If you are not sure what to focus on, become aware of a time in the relationship that you may have felt hurt, misunderstood, unloved, or confused. In my relationship with Kenni, the recurring pattern was a lack of good communication, his addiction, and my reaction to it.

Once you are aware of what you would like to resolve and heal, take responsibility for attracting and manifesting this situation. Accept that you experienced this condition or circumstance because your soul agreed to it. You may not know why you did or understand the lesson or purpose of experiencing this issue or challenge. It's not important that you figure that out right now.

Close your eyes, take a few long, deep cleansing breaths, and imagine an image of your loved one. Send him or her the mental thought and loving heart-centered message that you are releasing them from blame. Don't worry if you don't receive an intuitive response back—they will receive the message.

Although your loved one still must own their own actions, intent, thoughts, and behavior, take responsibility for your involvement. Accepting that you agreed to situations and conditions that caused you confusion or pain can be difficult. You may have felt unfairly treated, victimized, and that you did everything you could at the time to improve and heal the relationship. You may want the soul on the other side to acknowledge their role and ask for forgiveness, and it might take effort to shift out of the victim role.

You Have Agreed to Everything You Experience

You will never be powerless, or your well-being or happiness dependent on another, once you realize that everything you experience you have consented to. The conscious human you isn't fully able to understand this and will avoid taking any responsibility. Do it anyway, even if it makes no sense. The everyday self will likely feel overwhelmed with this idea. However, your soul and eternal essence sit squarely in this truth, and once you accept your participation, you begin to heal.

Although we often blame others, the root of what we experience in any relationship is within us. We carry our emotional patterns and wounds from lifetime to lifetime. The issues and challenges that we confront in one relationship are bound to show up in some form in others as well. We can leave a relationship only to find the same dissatisfying problems and issues crop up in the next one. The recurring patterns in our relationships are a reflection of where we need healing, love, and acceptance. Until we ask ourselves what our challenging relationships are trying to teach us, we are destined to repeat the same patterns.

When I accepted responsibility for my participation in what occurred during my marriage to Kenni, I still had no idea why I would have needed this lesson, and I didn't know what to do to heal. Slowly I began to realize that from the beginning of the relationship I knew that his drinking would be a problem. Still, I pushed aside my apprehension, put the blindfolds on, and held onto the false belief that our love would get us through. It didn't. Many of my relationships followed similar patterns. I had loose boundaries and ignored my needs and wanted to believe that love would be enough to sustain the relationship. I didn't clearly communicate my needs and desires and somehow assumed they were obvious. As I became aware of my contribution, I realized that these issues sprung from my wanting to please Kenni and my tendency to be in denial. I knew that for anything in my life to change, I had to change.

The idea that we have agreed to the experiences that come our way can incite anger and frustration. It's not easy to accept that we would knowingly allow difficulties into our lives. It is especially hard to accept that we would consent to a childhood where our parents or environment were detrimental to our mental, emotional, physical, and spiritual well-being.

However, we often choose and allow difficulties in our life as a path to compassion, increased spiritual awareness, and strength. A life of comfort doesn't always provide the stimulation we need to grow and evolve. Like an oyster that continually coats an irritating grain of sand until it becomes a pearl, friction opens us to deeper self-awareness and higher truths.

Suffering can silently carve out and refine our ability to be more compassionate and loving. Feeling unloved and alone can push us to open to a presence and power that transcends the physical world. It is often in our loneliness that we become aware of the love that exists within us and all around us. With this awareness comes the gift of strength and a transcendent power that allows us to reach out and help others.

When we accept that we are not a victim, we have a chance to break our unhealthy patterns and clear away the obstacles that hamper our ability to give and receive love. Otherwise we continue to unknowingly attract unsatisfying relationships and conditions that only bring more dissatisfaction. When we claim our power to consciously create, we step into freedom.

As you become more aware of the emotional patterns that have prevented you from fully loving and living in joy, be compassionate and gentle with yourself. Shame, guilt, confusion, and fear might surface as these patterns come to light. As challenging as it may be to feel these feelings, this begins the release process and is a sign that you are letting go of past pain, victimization, and limiting patterns.

We don't have to work on our issues alone. If need be, we can seek out help in healing from practitioners who are experienced in spiritual and emotional healing. A loving and compassionate friend or family member, as well as our loved ones on the other side, can also be of assistance.

As we open ourselves to the influence of the other side, we can transform with more ease, support, love, and grace. As our loved ones heal and experience higher states of love and wisdom, they reach out to us and can assist us with our own healing.

Letting Go of What You No Longer Need, Becoming Clear

The following meditation exercise will empower you to heal an emotional pattern that you experienced with a loved one who is now on the other side. No matter what the circumstances or conditions were that led to confusion, pain, or misunderstanding, you can let the suffering go and heal.

To begin, think of a recurring issue or confusing pattern that you experienced in a relationship with a loved one who is on the other side. You can use the same issue and loved one on the other side from the previous exercise. Write it down. Examples include such things as poor communication, combative arguments, falling out of love, jealousy, lack of effort, conflicting needs and wants, career issues or conflicts, or financial or sexual issues—any issue that created stress and misunderstanding.

Write down the emotions that this issue or concern tends to generate within you. Examples may be feelings such as pain, loneliness, low self-esteem, shame, anger, frustration, confusion, guilt, or fear.

Close your eyes, take a few deep, cleansing breaths, and imagine an image from the past when you experienced this particular issue or challenge with your loved one. As much as possible, feel the feelings that this challenge stirs up within you.

Breathe white light energy down through the top of your head and move this energy through the body. Continue to breathe in this way and invite your loved one on the other side to come close. Relax, breathe, open your heart, and speak your loved one's name or send them a thought or emotional message. Ask for them to help you heal and let go of the pain, confusion, and other emotional wounds from this pattern. You can also ask them to help you better understand and learn from this issue. Intend to let go of the pain or other feelings connected to this issue and allow healing love to enter.

As you become more relaxed, breathe white light down through the top of the head and exhale it through the heart. Continue to breathe in this way, exhaling through the heart. With each breath imagine your heart opening and any lingering pain, wounds, or other difficult emotions surfacing. Continue to breathe into your heart and allow and invite whatever needs to be healed to come forward. Pay attention to any sensations, thoughts, images, and feelings that surface.

Allow love to fill your heart and surround the inner emotional patterns, wounds, and limiting beliefs that are ready to be released with forgiveness, compassion, and acceptance. Breathe and imagine that you can now release these patterns. Ask your loved one from the other side to assist you in letting go. Invite their love and the higher love of the heavens to move through you. Let go and know that you are loved, forgiven, and cherished. Your wounds don't define you and they are not you. You are love and you are loved.

When you feel ready, thank those on the other side for their support and love, and open your eyes. Write down what you experienced in this meditation. As you write, allow any lingering feelings to surface.

During this meditation, you may feel the presence of a loved one and receive insights and new perspectives on your issue or challenge. It's also likely that you'll experience an emotional release and letting go. However, what you receive may not be fully discernible, or you may not experience or feel anything. If this happens, don't become discouraged. Healing is still occurring on a deep level. Quite often the true workings of the spirit realm are not consciously evident. In the coming days and weeks, pay attention to your dreams and intuition, as guidance may slowly drift in. You will also likely notice shifts in your sense of well-being and be less tired and burdened. While the same challenges and issues may still surface, you will find new ways to approach and resolve them.

Our loved ones on the other side have a lot to give. They will continue to send healing and do their best to respond to our requests. Through dreams, intuition, synchronicities, and being in the right place at the right time, we are often guided to the information, opportunities, and individuals that can help us to further heal.

Healing our relationships with those on the other side invigorates our soul. When we release and heal our unsatisfying emotional patterns, we vibrate to higher levels of pure love. In this higher vibration we are better able to connect with and feel our loved one's presence. When we heal relationships with those on the other side, we come into spiritual harmony with them and create positive change in our physical life.

Patterns that have been long standing, chronic, and difficult are lifted into the great love of spirit. In this high vibration energy, there is no time and space and no disharmony, negativity, or pain. Because emotional patterns are not individual but usually pass from generation to generation, healing not only benefits us—it also positively impacts our ancestors and future generations as well.

———

In the next chapter you'll discover more about the gifts that each relationship brings to you.

Chapter 13

Discovering a Relationship's Purpose and Gifts

On the other side we enjoy the full awareness of self. Our soul is aware of all the earthly actions, thoughts, emotions, and beliefs that have gotten in the way of our remembering who we are. In the physical world we don't always understand the importance of what we are experiencing.

It is always in our best interest to become more conscious and learn our lessons while still in the physical world. The progress we make here to heal our wounds, transform negative attitudes and beliefs, and act in loving ways, is not easy work. It requires self-discipline, determination, and the ability to become aware of our inner power and use it wisely. However, the progress we make here in the physical world seeps deep into our soul and is ours forever. This is real change and has big rewards here and on the other side.

Every relationship is a hot bed for soul growth and has a purpose. Like magnets, we are drawn to those who we connect with on a soul level. Our meeting with certain individuals in the physical life has been carefully orchestrated before our birth. An invisible soul current draws us to those we have a connection with.

While we move through our day-to-day issues and experiences, our soul is busy drawing to us the people, events, and circumstances that we most need to evolve and express love. Yet, we rarely fully recognize the soul significance of what we are experiencing, and it is not always necessary that we do. Masterfully weaving together events, relationships, and circumstances that provide us with the opportunity to increase our self-awareness and own our power, our soul knows what it's doing. We are with the people we need to be with and experiencing what is most important for us, even if it doesn't make sense at the time.

Emotions as Messengers

We are made whole by the divine invisible thread that binds us to one another. Through our interactions with others and the emotions and thoughts that they generate, we are better able to see and know who we are. Our connection with one another activates the power of our spirit.

At the core of all our relationships there is love, even when it seems the opposite. Those who you dislike, don't get along with, or rub you the wrong way serve a powerful purpose in your life. They, too, are divine messengers that draw out of you, often uncomfortably so, your truth and essence. Everyone you encounter brings you a gift, even though we rarely recognize it.

On the other side, we begin to understand the purpose and lessons that we have been learning and perfecting within our relationships. We are witness to the divine magic that has been behind everything we experienced in the physical world. As the truth of the path that we traveled in the physical life begins to take shape, we recognize that it is through the emotions and feelings we shared with another that we learn, heal, and evolve.

EXERCISE
Emotions That Teach

The following exercise and questions will help you join your loved one on the other side in learning through the emotional energy of a relationship.

To begin, bring to mind and heart your relationship with a particular loved one. Take a long, deep, relaxing breath, move it through the body, and exhale any stress or tension. Continue these cleansing breaths until you feel relaxed.

Imagine breathing white light energy down through the top of your head. Move this energy through the body and exhale through the heart. Continue to breathe in this way, opening your heart and allowing love to fill you. As you breathe and relax, imagine that your loved one is with you. They carry the light of love and healing in their heart and soul and offer it to you.

Continue to breathe and relax as you allow your heart to open and your mind to drift. Call to mind and heart past memories that you shared with your loved one. Welcome whatever memories come forward without consciously trying to make something happen.

Identify and feel the predominant feelings associated with the memories that surface. How did you feel in these memories with your loved one? Focus on the predominant feelings, write them down, and bring them into your full awareness.

As you continue to become aware of the predominate emotions you experienced in the relationship, ask yourself these questions:

- What does this feeling or emotion have to teach me?
- If my feelings had a voice and could speak, what would they be saying?
- What is the lesson that my soul is asking me to accept and learn through these emotions?
- How can I continue to love and support myself in relationships?
- Can I accept the love and healing being offered to me from my loved one and the higher divine?

Take your time, meditate on one question at a time, and breathe and listen within. Insights might come through thoughts, images, and a sense of knowing. Quite often the answers and awareness we intuitively seek don't immediately surface. If you did not receive the clarity that you had hoped for, continue to take time to ponder these questions, and all the answers and insights will come when you are ready to receive them.

As you continue to open yourself to the positive influence of the other side, send love and gratitude to your loved one in spirit for agreeing to take part in this experience with you and helping you to fulfill this purpose.

The Gift Within Relationships

Our influence and connection with our loved ones don't end at physical death. Once a loved one has passed over, we often gain renewed understanding and insights about them and ourselves. We also become more conscious of the gifts they gave us and our purpose together.

In addition to healing old patterns and freeing ourselves to more fully love self and others, relationships fulfill the purpose of helping us to more fully know who we are. Through the love of another, new aspects of our true nature come to life. Although relationships trigger limiting emotional patterns, they also call the higher qualities of love, compassion, forgiveness, and patience to flow through us. Within the synergy of our connection with another, new aspects of our divine nature ignite and come to life.

Some relationships support and encourage us to develop and fulfill a purpose that extends beyond the relationship and into the community or broader environment. For instance, through Kenni's addiction issues I was better able to understand and heal my relationship with my father. However, there was another gift that he brought into my life.

Except for a few years prior to our meeting, Kenni made his living as a musician. After we met, he went back to producing, writing, and playing music full-time. Devoted to his many musical projects, he was passionate about his work and took his creativity seriously. I quickly learned not to interrupt him when he was working. Even a little peek into his studio could elicit a "please leave me alone" look from him while I tiptoed out of the room.

I didn't share his creative devotion. For years I wanted to write, but it never felt like a good time. Something else always got my attention and seemed more important. I envied Kenni's commitment and continued to procrastinate and put off my own creative endeavors.

Then one afternoon while in the backyard playing with our dog, I felt the presence of a spirit nun near me. I didn't know who she was, but she had a strong message.

"It's time to write," she said.

When I tried to ignore her, she said it again. This time her attitude was a bit more like a commanding Mother Superior.

I didn't know if this was a request, suggestion, or command, but I took it seriously. It still took me a while to settle into writing, but I was in the perfect environment to commit to my creativity. Kenni cast an aura of creative focus and dedication, and I absorbed this supportive energy. I finished my first book that year and got to work on the next one.

When I look back on our time together, the contribution that Kenni made to my writing career is obvious. Still, I didn't realize the essential part he played until he passed over and started visiting me. As we reviewed our relationship, I realized the positive impact that his creative energy had on me.

EXERCISE
Relationship Questions for Contemplation

To embrace the influence that a relationship has had on supporting you or bringing a purpose to life, ask yourself these questions:

- While growing up, what abilities and talents did my family encourage and support?
- Was there a grandparent or other relative that noticed something special in me or influenced me through one of their own interests?
- What is easy and natural for me to give to others?
- What talents, habits, or attitudes do I admire in others that I would like to emulate?
- What relationship challenge or difficulty ultimately helped me be a better person?
- In what ways did a past relationship help me to move forward in my life?
- How has a relationship helped me in supporting or improving others' lives or the community?
- What qualities do my relationships most bring out in me?
- What positive characteristics do others see in me that I'm not always aware of?
- What has opened my heart to be of service to others?
- When do I feel the most joy in my relationships?

Ponder these questions and give yourself time to contemplate and come into greater awareness. Listen to your heart and the quiet intuitive voice of your soul. You may want to move slowly through each question and write down your thoughts in a journal. Eventually the gift of soulful insight will surface, bringing with it inspiration and a sense of renewal.

EXERCISE
Discovering Relationship Gifts

If you wonder what gift a particular relationship with someone on the other side offered you, call to mind this individual and ask for their presence.

Close your eyes and take a long, deep cleansing breath. Relax and exhale, release any stress and tension. Continue to breathe cleansing breaths and imagine an image of the person on the other side that you would like to communicate with. Speak their name, either silently or out loud.

Ask within for any memories to surface that contain insight into the gift of the relationship. Welcome any emotions that surface and allow them to unfold.

Feel the feelings connected to the memories and ask what you learned. If this is unclear, ask your loved one on the other side to communicate more information to you through thoughts, feelings, images, and insights.

Continue to send and receive messages through memories and insights with your loved one on the other side. Become aware of how the relationship helped you or opened new doors. How did the relationship change you? What can you see and understand now that you didn't know at the time?

In your current life, what might be different if this loved one had not been part of your life? What are you able to give to others and the world as a result of your relationship with your loved one who is now in spirit?

Let yourself move slowly through these questions. Open your heart and mind and be aware of what you receive intuitively. Sometimes you'll quickly come into more clarity and awareness as to the gifts that another has brought into your life, or this awareness will surface over time.

Your loved one on the other side might also share with you the gift that you brought into their life. They will do this through inner thought messages, images, feelings, and memories. Open your heart and allow yourself to receive whatever message your loved one has for you. When we try to control what we receive, we can easily get confused and miss out on the opportunity to feel the presence and love of our loved ones.

As with all the exercises and your attempts to communicate with the other side, be patient. Quite often the answers, information, and insights that you seek don't come through immediately. It can take some time for the messages to make their way into your conscious mind. Eventually they will, often when you least expect them and are not focusing on intuitively receiving information.

There may be no greater gift that this world offers than to be loved. From our human perspective, physical death is the end of an active and engaging love. What we have shared with our loved one may feel as if it has reached its finite conclusion. However, the gift that the relationship brings to life lives on long after a physical connection ceases.

———

In the next chapter you'll learn how your loved ones help you to move forward from the spirit realm.

Chapter 14
How Those on the Other Side Help Us to Move Forward

After a loved one passes over, we are confronted with the task of creating a new life. There is no way to prepare for the loss of another, or the loss of who we had been, when they are gone. Although our love and energetic connection to our loved ones never ceases, we can feel raw, vulnerable, and confused when they leave this world. In our shared synergy with a loved one, we became someone else, perhaps a more loving and confident self. When they are gone, we are left with the empty shell of our shared physical existence.

Perhaps the most difficult type of loss is that of a child. Our love and energetic bond with them is a part of our being. When they pass over, a part of us goes with them and we are forever transformed.

This is how Judy felt. Before I began the reading with her, she began to cry. I could feel her intense grief, and I could feel that she had suffered a tremendous loss. I sensed a spirit close whom I encouraged to come forward. When I did, he quietly whispered, and I wasn't able to understand what he was saying.

"Who are you talking to?" she asked.

"A young male, early twenties, wavy hair. He's coming through with a lot of emotion and wants you to know he's sorry... He's coming in stronger now and tells me that he is your son," I said.

With this, Judy put her head down and continued to cry.

I waited a few moments, as the emotional intensity was causing some static in our connection. As the energy cleared some, I was better able to connect with him.

"Your son wants you to know that you gave him a great life. He says it couldn't have been better. I get the impression you two were always very close," I said.

"When I lost Luke, I lost my heart," Judy said.

"I get the image of water, like a big lake. Your son is showing me a beautiful sunny day. It feels that he may have drowned. I see an ambulance and people running for help. He wants you to know that he's all right now and it's okay."

"Luke was never a strong swimmer. I guess he didn't realize how far out he got. They tried to resuscitate him, but it was too late. I love him and please let him know that I would rather be there with him than here on the earth without him," Judy said.

"Your son knows how much you love him. He can feel it in your heart. You can talk to him whenever you want; he can hear you," I said.

I continued to share messages for the remainder of the session. When we finished, Judy told me that every day she felt the pain of her son's passing.

"It's like I'm a ghost. I don't know who I am any longer. It feels as if there is a hole in me that will never be filled no matter what I do," she said.

Many clients who have lost loved ones share similar feelings of confusion and the awareness that they have also lost a part of themselves. As we move through the grief of loss, we discover that we are no longer the same person we were when our loved one was alive in the physical world. We, too, have changed and transformed, but we may not know who we are. Even though we may still live in the same familiar surroundings and go about our daily routines, we feel lost. Our friends may do their best to provide comfort and care, but there is no quick cure for grief. When we lose a loved one, it can feel as if an essential part of ourselves has been torn away. Confused, disoriented, and saddened, just getting through the day may be a challenge.

This is what is was like for Laura. After years of going back and forth, Laura and Dan finally agreed that it was time to buy a house in the mountains. After saving and paying off their cars and home, they decided to fulfill their dream of a mountain home.

After looking at properties all day one Saturday, they looked forward to a quiet evening watching the sunset from their hotel window. While Laura was drying off from a shower, she heard a groan and loud thud come from the bedroom. She called out to Dan, asking him if everything was okay, but didn't get a response. Entering the bedroom, she saw him spread out on the floor near the bed, gasping for air and going in and out of consciousness. She called for an ambulance and tried to administer CPR until they arrived.

Dan didn't last the night and never regained consciousness. He suffered a massive heart attack, and the doctors assured Laura that there was nothing she could have done to change the outcome.

Laura came in for a reading on a warm summer day several months later. When I began the reading, I quickly felt her husband's presence. Dan was talkative and thankful for the opportunity to speak to his wife. He described fond memories, gave other messages, and let her know that he had been reunited with their beloved poodle.

When I asked Laura if she had any questions, she opened her purse and took out a list. One by one, she went through questions that included everything from how to turn off the water heater to more spiritual and philosophical concerns such as, What is the meaning of life? What is God like?

Dan did his best to answer her questions, and we were close to being done with the session when Laura started to cry. Overwhelmed with the many decisions she now had to make on her own, she asked Dan if he could be with her and help her.

"I'm with you more than you know. I can feel your confusion and stress, and wish I could do more. Remember, every decision I made with work and in life in general I ran by you first. You always gave me the best advice. When you had a sense or gut feeling about something, I listened. Don't worry, just take it step by step," he said.

When our session ended, both Dan and Laura seemed to be more at peace.

I saw Laura again several months later and her grief and sorrow over losing Dan was still intense and at the forefront of her day-to-day life.

"I just can't seem to move forward," she said. "When Dan was here I was confident, and he's right: I usually did make good decisions and know what to do. Now, I don't even know what to buy in the grocery store or what to do about my finances. I haven't even paid any bills in a few months. This is so unlike who I was. How can I change so much? I don't know who I am anymore."

Like Laura, many feel as if what was once easy and second nature is now elusive and distant. We may sense and feel that we need to move forward but don't know how to go about it. Every relationship has a purpose and influences and impacts us in more ways than we might initially know.

The Surprising Souls That Guide Us

When a loved one passes over, we often have a lot of decisions to make. If the loved one is a close family member, we may need to make funeral arrangements and take care of such things as their finances and personal property. We might get overwhelmed with the demands and be focused on what needs to get done next. As the shock of the passing and the many things that needed tending to lessen, we are left with ourselves. Often lonely and still grieving, we try to figure out our next step and become aware of what needs attention in our own lives. We feel different and know that we have to rebuild our lives and find meaning and purpose, yet we seldom know where to begin.

In this confusion, we might find ourselves pondering such questions as: What is important in my life right now? What can I do or give that gives meaning to my life? Where am I going?

However, the answers we seek bypass logical thinking and defy past experiences. These questions are for the heart and soul, and the answers may seem to be out of our reach. Although we may look to others and the world for guidance, it is often our loved ones on the other side that offer the most insight and direction.

Although we feel alone and unable to decipher our next steps in life, our loved ones on the other side are close and aware of our challenges and the new life we are confronting. As they undergo the deep transformation of the other side, they become better able to know our thoughts, feel our feelings, and guide us along our soul path into happiness. Although we are not always aware of their efforts, the other side often plays an essential role in helping us to heal and move forward after their death.

The souls that guide and help us from the other side are not always the loved ones that we expect to be present. In addition to those we shared a loving, close, and trusting bond with, there are souls we may not have been close to in the physical life that offer the most help. Sometimes it is a child or even an unborn soul that we only knew through a pregnancy that is our closet spirit ally. Children who pass over and unborn souls often come into our physical lives for a brief visit to become closer to us. They may be angels and highly-evolved souls who have been with us since our birth, and love, guide, and protect us. Even though they retain their childlike nature on the other side for a time, their soul is ageless. It is from this higher soul awareness that they guide us.

The parents, family, and other loved ones who lose a child also chose to go through this experience to grow, learn, and more quickly evolve. As much as this doesn't make sense to our physical mind and heart, we agree to lives that involve illness, loss, and challenges. We do this to advance our evolution and refine our soul awareness. When we suffer, we are stripped down to the true marrow of life. The frivolous and empty ego-based longings and beliefs fall away. We have the opportunity to discover what is truly important and the power within us that transcends whatever is of this world. In the spirit realm we know who we are, and we never want to lose this awareness and connection to divine source.

All too often we earthlings strive for lives of physical comfort and ease, and we cling to illusions of false power and self-importance. If we are consumed by these types of desires and worldly goals, we may ignore our heart and spiritual calling. The soul doesn't make progress and can experience inertia and become stagnant. The way of all life, physical and non-physical, is change, activity, and evolution. It is the unfurling of our soul into full expression that brings us joy.

Our Children as Guides

Losing a loved one, especially a child, is usually a part of your soul contract with them. Before we make our way into the physical life, we devise a plan that encourages our growth and supports our soul's purpose. Advanced and loving souls may agree to come into this life to provide us with the opportunity to make rapid soul advancement. Our bond with them is stronger than physical death. When they pass over, a pathway for continued connection, communication, and guidance opens up. Blessings, love, and positive energy flow to us from our loved one who has transitioned to the other side.

Shannon, a young mother, is the recipient of this kind of spiritual love. When she came in for a reading, I immediately noticed her gentle nature. She seemed a little nervous and told me that she had never had a reading. We got started and her grandmother on the other side came in right away. She seemed concerned and worried about Shannon and wanted her to know that she was close and looking after her. There was a young spirit girl by her side, and I realized that this was Shannon's daughter.

"Do you have a blue-eyed young daughter with dark hair on the other side? She looks to be about ten or eleven. She's thin and must have had a long-term illness," I said.

"That's Katie and she had a kidney condition since birth," Shannon said.

"Your daughter has such a sweet, gentle spirit. I think she's an angel—not *like* an angel—but an angel. She's close and wants you to know she always will be. If you catch the scent of flowers, this is her."

"It's funny you say this. I came in the house a few nights ago and the smell of roses was so strong, I thought maybe I was imagining it."

"Your daughter is showing me an image of a man who has blond hair and a thick build. I get the impression that this is not her father but someone you were in a relationship with. She says that she is proud of you. It feels like you ended the relationship; is this true? It was difficult for you to walk away, but you did. It feels like she helped you to do this," I said.

"Soon after Katie's passing, I was so lonely, and I couldn't find myself. I don't know why but I started dating a man that I knew wasn't right for me. All the signs were there that it wasn't going to work, but he seemed to fill the hole in my heart or maybe just distracted me from it. He fits the description. How did she help me with this? Sometimes I feel stronger, like a wave of love flows through my heart. Could this be her?" Shannon asked.

"It's likely that this is your daughter giving you strength and helping you. She says that she came into your physical life to be closer to you and was never here to live a long life. She's aware of your soul path and can send you love and positive thoughts and support you in ways that you may never be able to fully detect and know. It's your job to listen and trust the small nudges and intuition that point you toward the positive. Your daughter is devoted and will always be with you," I said.

Help from Those We Had Difficulties With

After passing over, many souls stay close to their loved ones here in the physical world to fulfill aspects of their soul contract with them. Most provide us with unconditional love and comfort and often essential guidance. However, there are times when a loved one must fulfill a responsibility or commitment that they agreed to in their soul contract but did not follow through on in the physical life. When an individual exercises their free will and veers away from the role that they had agreed to play with another, they may not fully realize it until they pass over. In the lucid awareness of the spirit realm, they come face-to-face with the folly of their actions.

During the soul review our loved ones become aware of and feel the effect that their actions, words, or attitudes have had on others. They also become aware of how their actions have impacted their heart and soul purpose. For instance, if a parent has a soul contract to love and support a child and they instead allow their ego, fears, or desire for less responsibility dictate their behavior, they must confront this in the soul review. The soul contract often includes such things as learning how to put aside personal desires, compromise, and supporting others.

Unfinished and unresolved relationship issues are being addressed on the other side. Where there has been misunderstanding there is now awareness; love replaces hate, and fear and negativity are transformed into positivity. Whenever there has been neglect, disregard, addiction, or abuse from a family member or friend who is now in spirit, you can be sure that active healing is taking place. The impact that they had on you is part of the soul review and amends, forgiveness, and transformation are occurring. You are the beneficiary of their renewed perspective, as they must now influence your life in helpful, loving, and positive ways.

When our loved ones fail to fulfill their soul responsibilities, they have the opportunity to practice them from the spirit realm. Pulled by love and the newfound awareness of how their actions may have adversely impacted others, those on the other side learn that they can focus their attention and efforts toward helping, guiding, and comforting their loved ones in the physical world. They learn that they can practice being a good father, mother, spouse, or other family member from the other side. It is never too late to make amends and learn and practice selfless love.

Ancestral Guidance

Ancestors and family members that we didn't know in the physical world can also be unlikely but effective spirit helpers. Quite often they have been with us since birth, guiding, loving, and helping us in a variety of ways. When they come forward in a reading, my client is often surprised, as they may have only a faint recollection of who they are.

Our ancestors are aware of the family patterns that may be unconsciously influencing us and how our choices and actions can create a ripple effect from one generation to the next. Many of our ancestors see the devastating and unsatisfying effects of the past and want to help free us from it.

Every so often a grandparent, great-grandparent, or another family member from generations back comes forward in a reading. Their interest and the inspiration to assist us is usually motivated by similarities that we share with him or her. We might unknowingly struggle with the same emotional patterns and share similar issues with addiction or health problems. However, our ancestors often come forward to assist and guide us in abilities and talents that they, too, developed and enjoyed.

For instance, Tatum, whose father had recently passed over, came in for a session. After speaking with her father for most of the session, I began to see and feel another male spirit close to him. I knew he was a family member, but I couldn't identify exactly who he was. He told me that he was her grandfather, but he wore clothing from a past century and I realized he was from a few generations past.

"I believe this is your great-grandfather or maybe an ancestor from even further back. He was from another country; it feels like he came here from Ireland. I see an image of him as a younger male; he's working hard, physical labor. I get the impression that he wanted to come to this country to go to school and did everything he could to save money. Are you in medical school? I get the impression from him that he was interested in medicine and you might be too."

"My father used to talk about his father's grandfather who came here from Ireland. I'm so glad he's with him. My father spoke lovingly of him. He wanted to be a doctor, but I don't think he ever did. I guess he had to drop out to support the family," Tatum said.

"Well, he's proud of you for pursuing medical school and wants to help you succeed," I said. "He knows it's hard to focus on studying while you grieve your father's passing and wants you to know he's doing all he can to help you out. He's showing me an image of himself whispering in your ear while you take exams. I think he's trying to slip you some answers."

"Oh, that's interesting. I have been concerned about exams. I've been so sad and it's been hard to focus and study. Last week I was sure I was going to do poorly on an exam, and I was so surprised when answers just seemed to pop into my head. I wonder if that's him?"

"I think it may be; he seems determined to help you through this," I said.

Our loved ones on the other side help us in ways that defy logic and explanation. While grieving for the loss of a loved one, we are often not ourselves and might become forgetful, make bad relationship decisions, have accidents, not take care of our health, and act in other uncharacteristic ways. Those on the other side are aware of where we may need help and may nudge and remind us to take care of ourselves in even the mundane day-to-day details of life.

Common Ways the Other Side Guides Us

As our loved ones move through the soul review and settle into the spirit realm, they tenderheartedly reach out to help us through the difficult passage of loss. Love, support, guidance, and assistance with moving forward come from those who were close to you and are now in the spirit realm. The love that you shared with your parents, spouse, children, and others is strong and vibrant on the other side.

When we are struggling or feeling sad and alone, our loved ones are by our side, whispering in our ear, holding our hand, or quietly sitting by our bed or next to us on the couch. They don't care if we know they are with us, and they may not have a particular message. They often simply hold us in love and warmth to ease our pain. In addition to offering us comfort and love, our friends and family in the spirit realm often guide us in moving forward in surprising ways. Never underestimate the power of a loved one on the other side to create miracles in our life.

It is not necessary to consciously know who is helping us and how and what they are doing to assist. Those on the other side don't always need to be known or acknowledged, as they experience positive vibrations of joy through being of service and enhancing our well-being. They know that we are confronting a new life, and they often come up with clever and creative ways to guide us.

Here a few of the more common ways they draw close:

Dreams

When we are lost and don't know how to go forward, our loved ones might send us messages of inspiration, hope, and new possibilities through our dreams. In these messages they may remind us of talents, hopes, and aspirations from our past that we may have set aside or describe possible new interests that speak to our heart and soul. These dreams may be symbolic, and even though we may not be able to fully decipher them, we may wake feeling more inspired or motivated.

For instance, a year and a half after her mother's passing, Brenda felt unmotivated and listless. After being by her mother's side during her long illness, Brenda no longer had a sense of purpose and felt unfocused now that she was gone. One night she dreamt that she was in a field thick with fog. She saw a ray of light and followed it to a garden where she saw her mother on her knees pulling weeds. When her mother turned, she had a warm and radiant smile.

Waking up from the dream, Brenda felt better than she had in a long time. She knew that her mother was happy and at peace. Later that day as she sat and looked out her window at the remnants of her own garden, she realized what a long time it had been since she had taken care of it. She felt her mother nudge her and she went outside and got to work. As she cleaned the flower beds, buried emotions of sadness surfaced. After she allowed herself a good cry, warm feelings of hope slowly trickled into her heart. As she pulled the last of the weeds, new insights and ideas about her future unexpectedly sprung up, and she felt her spirits come back to life.

Telepathic Thoughts

On the other side, we communicate through telepathy. This is the ability to send and receive thought messages through intent. It is like speaking to someone without using your voice.

Have you ever had an inspiring thought that motivates you with a new idea or suggestion to try something new? Those on the other side often send us guiding messages this way. Yet, we seldom recognize these telepathic thoughts as coming from the spirit realm. Instead, it usually feels as if we generate them on our own. Rarely do these spirit thoughts sound or feel different from our normal inner voice.

Thought messages from the other side are usually even toned, calm, persistent, and repetitive. They don't scream or shout or cause us anxiety or stress. Quite often they emerge while we are doing something relaxing and mundane like folding laundry, cooking, or listening to music. Our loved ones often take advantage of quiet moments when we are sitting at the kitchen table looking out the window, lounging outside on a deck or patio, or leisurely driving a familiar route to speak to us.

Pay attention to the quiet and persistent thoughts that seem to float into your awareness; the more often you recognize those that you suspect might contain a message, the more you receive and are better able to decipher.

Opportunities

Although we rarely recognize their intervention, our loved ones on the other side may bring opportunities our way. Sometimes we find ourselves in the right place at the right time to meet someone who positively impacts or helps us in some way. Doors to adventures and new possibilities might unexpectedly swing open, even when it seems unlikely or against the odds.

For instance, my son's friend Rich had a lifelong dream to go to the prestigious college that his grandfather attended. Even with his good grades and stellar recommendations, he knew that admittance was not guaranteed. When the long-awaited letter from the school arrived, he was disappointed to learn that he been put on the wait-list. His beloved grandfather had died just a few months prior to receiving the letter, and he was sad that he wouldn't be attending the same college.

Later that day while walking his dog, he found two shiny pennies in the heads-up position on his path. When he was a child his grandfather would give him pennies for good luck, and he knew that finding them in the heads-up position was especially significant. For the next several weeks he continued to find pennies and every time he did, he thought of his grandfather.

One afternoon he opened his mailbox and saw another letter from the college. Before opening it, he knew that this was an acceptance letter. As he read the positive news, he thanked his grandfather.

Heartfelt Emotions

On the other side, love is like air. It is the vital life force energy that sustains us and nurtures and supports our energy body. Those on the other side often send us guiding messages through positive feelings and heart-centered loving warmth.

If you are feeling lost and don't know where to go or what to do after the loss of a loved one, let your heart guide you. What are you drawn to? What gets your attention or brings you a feeling of warmth and joy? Follow the feelings of what helps you feel good. You don't have to figure out the future or know where you are going. Try new things and if they don't feel good, move on to something else. Moment to moment, trust your heart to guide you.

Your loved ones encourage you to open your heart and allow the soft and warm healing vibrations of love in. They often do this by bringing the people and conditions your way that will make your heart smile.

Heavenly Matchmaking

Love and relationships on the other side are not like they are here on earth. There is no jealousy, ego, expectations, or possessiveness. With our expanded spiritual understanding and vision, we experience love as freedom and joy. The love that we have for our partners and spouse transforms into a soulful eternal bond that isn't restrictive or confining. Instead, it is part of who we are and supports us in our sacred journey into our true self.

When I do a reading for someone who has lost their spouse or partner, they sometimes wonder if it would upset them if they loved another. This is never the case. Once on the other side, your loved one only wants what is best for you. They don't want you to be lonely and without a partner to share your love with.

Not only does our spouse, partner, boyfriend, or girlfriend want us to be loved and cared for, they often send people our way and help us open our heart and allow another in. Our loved ones might encourage us to become more social, volunteer, or join a group activity. Sometimes a special friend with whom we find companionship and comfort comes our way, and they might even send us another soul mate or life partner.

This is what happened with Della, whom I first met on a cold February morning. She seemed to be in her late thirties and quietly sat across from me. Soon after I began the session, a man in spirit came forward.

"There is a dark-haired man, about six feet tall, average build, who is standing near you. I can feel love radiating from him to you. This must be a husband or partner," I said.

"It's my husband, Ray," Della said.

For the next forty minutes, Ray shared messages about the business they built together and their two young children.

I was just about to ask Della if she had any questions for Ray when he interrupted.

"Your husband is saying that you won't be alone for long," I said.

"What? Is Ray saying that I'm going to be in another relationship? I don't see that happening. I'm busy with our children and with work. Besides, I have no interest; Ray was the love of my life," Della said.

She looked confused, and so I asked Ray to share more.

"He says that he wants you to have someone in your life who will love and care for you and the children. Keep your heart and mind open," I said.

Della didn't say much, and we went on to other issues.

Two years after this session, I saw Della again. We began the reading and once again Ray came forward. When I told Della this, she told me that she wanted to know if he was upset with her. She didn't tell me why and when I asked him this, he started to laugh.

"He's not upset with you; he's laughing. Ray is showing me a man…I get the feeling that you met someone. Ray says that he helped make this happen and he likes him."

"That's a relief, I was worried that Ray might think that I don't love him or that I've forgotten about him. I don't know how this all works," Della said.

"I can assure you that Ray loves you and is happy you're not alone," I said.

After a short pause, Della continued, "I met Chuck, my new friend, at a bereavement support group. I didn't want to go, but I felt stuck and a friend pushed me to go. We met at the first meeting, sat next to one another. His wife died around the same time that Ray did, same hospital in fact. He has a daughter about my daughter's age…We're getting very close. You sure Ray seems okay with this?"

"More than okay; he says he's relieved and he loves you. He doesn't want you and the kids to be alone. He says that Chuck is a good man."

Synchronicities

Those on the other side can be tricksters who like to play and surprise us. One of the most common ways they do this is through synchronicity or unexpected coincidence. The spirit realm is quite masterful at getting our attention through such things as sending us recurring numbers, specific birds, butterflies, or other natural phenomena like meaningful cloud formations or rainbows. They might also send us guiding messages through hearing a particular song either in our external environment or through inner hearing. In addition, if you repeatedly come across or hear the name of a doctor or other health practitioner, accountant, or other professional, this might be a synchronistic sign you need to pay attention to.

Our loved ones on the other side can put us in the right place at the right time to meet the people who may be able to help or benefit us in some way. They also might bring others to us that we can learn from and discover new interests and aspects of ourselves. Sometimes we meet others through synchronistic encounters who we can influence and help and discover that we have more to give than we were aware of.

When you encounter or notice a synchronicity, open your heart and mind to its significance. Try not to overthink and become discouraged if you can't quickly discern its message. It may take some time to become aware of the direction or guidance it brings your way. When we are unable to recognize the meaning of a synchronicity, another one often comes to emphasize or repeat its message. Your loved ones are patient and will continue to send you guiding messages and signs in a variety of ways.

If you feel as if you've received a guiding sign or message from a loved one on the other side, do your best to act on it. Messages from the other side don't always come with lengthy and convincing explanations or a map of the future. Even if you don't fully understand the significance of what you are receiving, take a step forward in faith.

After the loss of a loved one, it can take time to discover who we are and what gives meaning and purpose to our lives. Without our loved one's reflection of warmth and love, we may feel like a flower in search of the sun when it is hidden behind dense clouds. There is no one way to go forward after a loss. Let yourself be led and be willing to explore. Try new things, and if you discover that something is not for you, move on to something else. Give yourself permission to be like a young child in pursuit of new experiences such as art and dance classes, play dates, and all kinds of activities and pursuits. There is not a right or wrong approach; allow the spirit of exploration and curiosity to guide you. Eventually you will find a renewed sense of purpose. Some find that pursuing new activities—such as helping and being of service to those in need, creative pursuits, social or travel opportunities, or a new line of work—are helpful in meeting new people and becoming better acquainted with themselves. That you are still here on this earth means that there is something more for you to learn, experience, give, receive, and share with others.

Epilogue

The Way of the Heavens

Although the words *mourning* and *morning* are pronounced the same, they have two very different meanings. Mourning describes a period of grief and sorrow after a loss. When in mourning, we are in a transformative passage where we confront, experience, and feel the immensity of the loss of our loved one and our lives without them.

In contrast, morning is the beginning of a new day. As the light of the sun slowly creeps up high into the sky, we often anticipate with hope what the day will bring our way. While mourning is often thought of as a time of emotional darkness, it is the morning that brings light.

However, in some ways, mourning can also bring a new beginning. Grieving and letting go of our loved one wakes us to a new life. Even though we would rather still have our loved one by our side, we are introduced to life without them. As we mourn and go through the many stages of grief and loss, we may feel emotionally, mentally, and spiritually fragile. Our heart and soul often feel torn and tattered and the skies empty and vacant. Emotions and aspects of ourselves that we may not be too familiar with come to the forefront.

Along with the profound inner challenges that grief brings our way, we are often confronted with very worldly demands. If we've lost a partner, spouse, or loved one that was part of our everyday life, we have to develop new routines and figure out how to take care of things on our own. There are financial, social, and other decisions to be made, and we might feel overwhelmed and unable to negotiate our way through them. Accompanying the day-to-day challenges, we are also being pulled and swayed by emotions and feelings that may seem to have a life of their own. In grief we learn that we cannot control what we feel and must instead trust the process and follow what grief asks of us.

As the process of mourning unfolds, our desire to feel close to our loved one on the other side and know if they are perhaps with us continues unabated. Soon after a loved one passes over, there may be moments when we feel their presence close by. We might also dream of our loved ones and notice signs and synchronicities that we suspect they might have sent our way. The heartbreaking shock of loss can also intensify our intuitive awareness. We may suddenly know information without knowing how we know it, experience penetrating and accurate intuitive insights, and receive thought messages and communication from our loved ones. Some begin to dream of spiritual places and divine beings or experience other ethereal encounters.

It is also equally likely that however much we long to feel the presence of our loved ones, we don't feel anything. For some, the intensity of grief can act as a static barrier, preventing clear, intuitive receptivity. Not being able to feel or sense the presence of our loved ones can be distressing. However, they are with us even when we can't sense or feel them. As the overwhelming shock of loss lessens, our intuitive ability usually becomes clearer and more accessible, and it becomes easier to tune in to their presence.

Slowly from the darkness of loss, a morning of sorts rises from within the depths of our heart and soul. We become more hopeful that perhaps new adventures await us both in the world and with our loved one on the other side. From the clear skies of light and open space, we begin to anticipate the arrival of messages and signs and the feel of love and warmth from our loved ones on the other side.

Becoming One with Our Loved Ones

To encourage continued intuitive growth and awareness and the strengthening of your bond with your loved one on the other side, review the material in this book from time to time. As you do, you'll gain new insights, notice intuitive information you may have missed, or derive new meaning and understanding from what you have read. As you become more aware of how to recognize your loved one's presence, your confidence in your ability to detect when they are close and discern their messages expands.

In time it will be natural to feel your loved one with you. You may find yourself carrying on an inner heart or thought conversation with him or her. Perhaps while going about your day you might recognize a familiar sign they send your way in an attempt to let you know they are close. Ever expanding and evolving, our intuitive connection with our loved ones is fluid, and some days it will be clearer and more accurate than others.

Be aware that many find that as they settle into an intuitive connection with their loved one on the other side, unexpected changes in intuitive awareness occur. After going along for some time feeling assured of a consistent and tangible intuitive bond with a loved one, we may no longer be able to clearly feel their presence and connect with them. Sometimes this change happens slowly over a period of time, or it may occur more quickly. Either way, it may cause concern and confusion.

People often come to me concerned that they no longer feel their loved one's presence, and they don't understand why. They may have previously been aware of when a loved one was present, noticed signs they sent their way, and had a fairly clear sense of the meaning within their messages. Then all of sudden this seems to fade. Stress and fear may surface as they wonder if their loved ones have moved on and are no longer with them.

This kind of shift in intuitive awareness is common and natural. As our loved ones continue to evolve on the other side, our energetic and love connection also transforms. Although it can be disconcerting to not be able to feel them close by or in our home or environment, they are still with us. This phenomenon occurs as the synergy that we share with our loved ones ascends into the higher vibrations of love.

During this shift we may no longer experience their presence outside and around us. Instead, they are felt more deeply from within our heart and soul. This is the gift of oneness and can occur soon after the passing of a loved one or years later.

For instance, Rose, whom I have given several readings to, shared a loving and meaningful bond with her grandmother. When her grandmother quietly passed over, Rose was distraught and wanted to know that she had made it into the light. Rose wanted to be assured that her grandmother was with other family members who had previously passed over and was being loved and cared for. After spreading her grandmother's ashes over the clear water of a mountain lake, Rose came in for a reading.

When I began the session, I saw an image of Rose walking down a path in the forest. The soft green leaves of tall trees surrounded her, and little spring shoots of flower buds sprang up from the earth. Soaking in the serenity and quiet of the environment, a ray of sunlight seemed to be guiding her. There was a peacefulness that I could feel with her that seemed to be in contrast to the stress that I usually felt coming from Rose during sessions. Her heart was open and emanated a warmth and wisdom.

After sharing this with Rose, I felt her grandmother close and turned my attention to continue the reading and communicate with her. When I began to intuitively tune in to her grandmother's energy, I realized that the feelings of peace, loving warmth, and wisdom I was experiencing were coming from her. Although it felt as if I was reading Rose's energy, the path in the forest that I saw Rose walking through, and the feelings of peace I felt, were actually what her grandmother was experiencing on the other side. Suddenly it occurred to me that Rose's grandmother was not just close to Rose, she was within her. Nestled in Rose's heart, her grandmother had become one with her.

When our loved one's energy merges with ours, the subtle feelings of love and wisdom from the other side are more accessible. This merging of energies takes place when our souls have attained a level of peace with one another. Our heart and souls meet in the river of love and we flow in unison. However, we still retain our individuality and our unique soul purpose and expression. When we listen to our heart, we are guided to our greater good through the soft, otherworldly humming presence of the heavens.

You Are Here for a Purpose

The message of the other side is simple. Beyond the ego needs, fears, and desires, there is perfect love that you are a part of and is always with you. There is no death, and ultimately everything comes into its most true expression of love, wholeness, and deep joy.

Your life has purpose, and there are powerful spirit beings guiding you every step of the way, although the mass hypnosis of the physical world may make it hard to always know, feel, and believe this. Listen within and trust the whispers of your heart. Your loved ones are always present and available to help you find your way back into the nirvana and joy of your true essence.

Your presence here on earth is essential and a magnificent gift. There is still something here for you to experience, do, learn, give, and share. No one can tell you exactly what this is. The awareness of the personal and sacred contract that exists between you and your creator comes from within.

It's easy to sometimes forget the beauty of our journey here on earth and the opportunity that it presents for us to experience the masterful and divine creative activity that we are a part of. Do what makes you happy and brings you joy; this is the way of the heavens.

Prayers

Allow the soul journey with your loved one to continue to unfold. In the physical world our connection with others winds through the everyday and mundane and only hints of eternity. When a loved one passes over, our connection with them continues in the whispers and light touch of their presence. However, in this physical world, and in the life beyond, our love is ruled by the light that is always present, shining, and nurturing for all beings.

Prayer is a lifting up of our spirit into this wise, loving presence of the divine all that is. It is an avenue through which we can find solace and invoke blessings and peace for ourselves and our loved ones. The following prayers and meditations may help you to open your heart and sink deep into the soulful love and presence that you share with those on the other side. Peace and blessings be with you.

Prayer for Passing Over

Divine Presence of Light, guide my loved one to the shores of all love and peace. Send me a beam of your golden light, and bury it deep into my heart and soul. Extend this golden light into the heart of my loved one and bind us together for all of eternity in your pure love and light. Let my loved one know of my unceasing love and devotion and grant us peace.

Prayer of Grief

Mother, Father Divine, my heart has sunk deep into the bottomless reservoirs of grief. Allow the depths of this sadness to reach into the pure divine heart and wipe clean my soul of all that is not love. As tears of loss move through me, let them bear witness to every moment of love I share with my loved one. Then allow my tears to dissolve into the vast sea of formless existence, where my loved one rises in joy.

Prayer for Moving On

Divine Presence, in the timelessness and formlessness of pure existence, my loved one travels. My loved one has become like a star in the dark night. I reach out and yet they seem so distant. Gather me into your arms and bring me to the doorway of all love.

My loved one is here and nowhere simultaneously. How do I know when they are near; do they hear my words and feel my love? Where do we meet face-to-face, heart-to-heart? How do I live in this world as if every day is real and holds meaning? Whisper these truths to my soul and reveal the divine path forward.

Prayer for a Child

Divine light of all love, lift my child into your heart. Hold their hand and lead them into the garden of peace and joy. Let them rest among the beauty of endless skies and flowers that whisper smiles. Watch over their tender heart and see to it that they know that they are loved beyond any kind of love that this world has known. Allow them to play, learn, and grow in ways that they could not in this physical land of shadows. Keep them safe, warm, and forever in your holy gaze.

Prayer for Healing and Restoration

Holy one, you who are forever the bearer of compassion and love, heal my loved one. Where once they stumbled and could not walk, let them run and dance in the light of an endless sun. Transform their suffering into endless joy and erase from their memory the sadness and pain. Let all that was denied them in this life be offered in boundless abundance.

Your divine presence is like the fragrant scent of spring and fresh blossoms moving through the soul. Let raindrops of love shower my loved one with bliss.

Prayer when Feeling Lost

Divine Mother Goddess, help me to find my way; I'm lost. There is darkness wherever I look. When my loved one departed, a light was extinguished from this world. Let me absorb their essence and feel the soft touch of their love once more. You who are all-eternal, show me kindness and soothe away my doubt and fear. Let me see and be as you and cross the wide expanse of time and space to rest in the love of those held in your grasp.

Prayer of Forgiveness

Brilliant light of love, allow my loved one to huddle close to your heart of compassion. In the divine presence, all is seen and known. Please send the angel of forgiveness to my loved one and wrap them in the wings of transformation. Forgive their misdeeds, mistakes, and all they did that was not of love. Then send this angel to me and purify my soul so that my loved one can find a haven and rest in my heart.

Prayer for Joy

Divine Mother, you are the bridge from fear to joy, from death to life, from being to nonbeing. Take me with you into eternity and reveal to me the truth of life. In your light, death is an illusion, and the petty shadows of doubt clear from my eyes. I want to see as you and be forever in the world of light. Grace my days with joy and not sorrow, fill my heart with the truth of existence, and always hold me close to those I love who eternally play in your soft gaze.

Bibliography and Recommended Reading List

Beattie, Melody. *The Language of Letting Go: Daily Meditations for Codependents.* Center City, MN: Hazelden, 1990.

Brennan, Barbara Ann. *Hands of Light: A Guide To Healing Through the Human Energy Field.* New York: Bantam, 1988.

Chödrön, Pema. *When Things Fall Apart: Heart Advice For Difficult Times.* Boulder, CO: Shambhala, 2016.

Dass, Ram. *Be Here Now.* San Cristobal, NM: Hanuman Foundation, 1978.

Dillard, Sherrie. *I've Never Met A Dead Person I Didn't Like: Initiation by Spirits.* Winchester, UK: John Hunt Publishing, 2019.

Dillard, Sherrie. *You Are A Medium: Discover Your Natural Abilities to Communicate with the Other Side.* Woodbury, MN: Llewellyn Publications, 2013.

Eden, Donna and David Feinstein. *Energy Medicine: Balancing Your Body's Energies for Optimal Health, Joy, and Vitality.* New York: Little Brown Group, 2013.

Hanh, Thich Nhat. *The Miracle of Mindfulness: An Introduction to the Practice of Meditation.* Translated by Mobi Ho. Boston, MA: Beacon Press, 1999.

Kübler-Ross, Elisabeth, and David Kessler. *On Grief and Grieving: Finding the Meaning of Grief Through the Five Stages of Loss.* New York: Scribner, 2014.

Lennox, Michael. *Dream Sight: A Dictionary and Guide for Interpreting Any Dream.* Woodbury, MN: Llewellyn Publications, 2011.

Myss, Caroline. *Anatomy of the Spirit: The Seven Stages of Power and Healing.* New York: Harmony Books, 2013.

Newton, Michael. *Destiny of Souls: New Case Studies of Life Between Lives.* St. Paul, MN: Llewellyn Publications, 2000.

Orloff, Judith: *Emotional Freedom: Liberate Yourself from Negative Emotions and Transform Your Life.* New York: Harmony Books, 2010.

Osho. *Buddha: His Life and Teachings and Impact on Humanity.* San Fransisco, CA: OSHO Media International, 2010.

Riggs, Nina. *The Bright Hour: A Memoir of Living and Dying.* New York: Simon and Schuster, 2017.

Rinpoche, Sogyal. *The Tibetan Book of Living and Dying.* San Francisco, CA: Harper Collins, 2012.

Ruiz, Miguel and Janet Mills. *The Four Agreements: A Practical Guide to Personal Freedom (A Toltec Wisdom Book).* With Janet Mills. San Rafael CA: Amber-Allen Publishing, 1997.

Rumi, Jala al-Din. *The Essential Rumi.* Translated by Coleman Barks with John Moyne, A.J. Arberry, and Reynold Nicholson. New York: Castle Books, 1997.

Schwartz, Robert. *Your Soul's Plan: Discovering the Real Meaning of the Life You Planned Before You Were Born.* Berkeley, CA: Frog Books, 2009.

Tolle, Eckhart. *A New Earth: Awakening to Your Life's Purpose.* New York: Penguin, 2008.

Weiss, Brian L. *Many Lives, Many Masters: The True Story of a Prominent Psychiatrist, His Young Patient, and the Past-Life Therapy That Changed Both Their Lives.* New York: Simon and Schuster, 1988.

Wallis Budge, E. A. *The Egyptian Book of the Dead: The Papyrus of Ani in the British Museum.* Mineola, New York: Dover Publications, 1967.

Zukav, Gary. *The Seat of the Soul.* New York: Simon and Schuster, 2007.

To Write to the Author

If you wish to contact the author or would like more information about this book, please write to the author in care of Llewellyn Worldwide Ltd. and we will forward your request. Both the author and publisher appreciate hearing from you and learning of your enjoyment of this book and how it has helped you. Llewellyn Worldwide Ltd. cannot guarantee that every letter written to the author can be answered, but all will be forwarded. Please write to:

Sherrie Dillard
⁄ Llewellyn Worldwide
2143 Wooddale Drive
Woodbury, MN 55125-2989

Please enclose a self-addressed stamped envelope for reply,
or $1.00 to cover costs. If outside the U.S.A., enclose
an international postal reply coupon.

Many of Llewellyn's authors have websites with additional
information and resources. For more information,
please visit our website at http://www.llewellyn.com